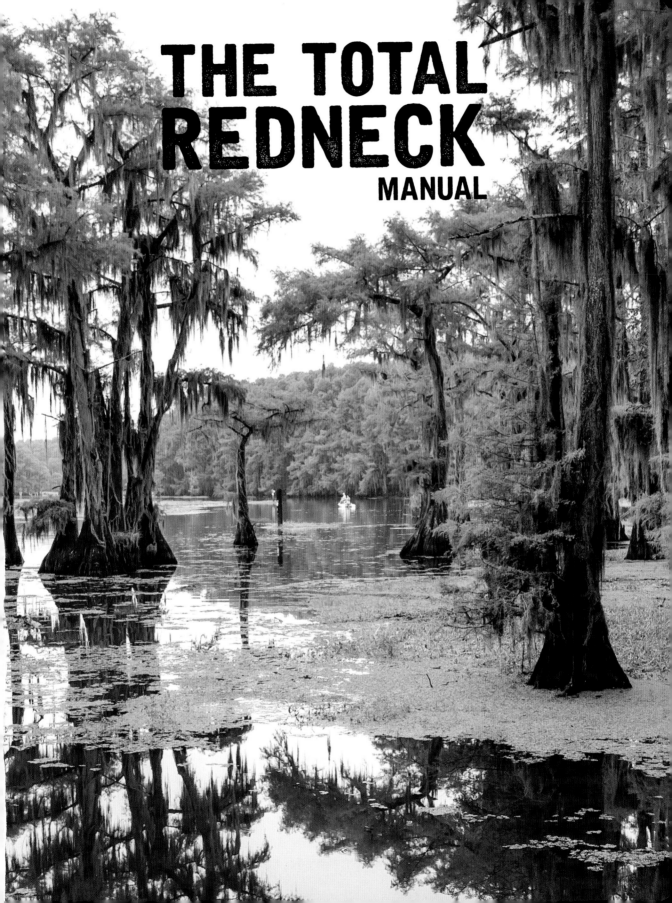

THE TOTAL
REDNECK
MANUAL

FIELD&STREAM

THE TOTAL REDNECK MANUAL

T. EDWARD NICKENS
and WILL BRANTLEY

weldonowen

FROM THE EDITOR

Growing up, every Christmas my brothers and I could each count on receiving a calendar from our parents. One year, the calendar I got was Jeff Foxworthy's "You Might Be a Redneck . . ."

After unwrapping the calendar, I read a few of the pages to my family, and we laughed a good bit. The wisecracks were funny at first, but by early February, they lost their bite. The jokes were repetitive, but what truly grew tiresome was the routine, day after day, of one-liners with one goal: making fun of caricatures.

When you have the good fortune of crossing paths with a true redneck—and, trust me, you'll know it—take notes, because they can teach you a thing or two about manners, humor, work ethic, family values, and, of course, hunting and fishing. After all, you don't burn the back of your neck without killing a ton of time outdoors.

The authors of this book, T. Edward Nickens and Will Brantley, are two such rednecks; in the years I've known them, I've learned plenty. I killed my first deer and wood duck with Eddie, and I've chased Kentucky gobblers and skinned catfish with Will. With both of them, I've enjoyed a good bit of bourbon and howled in laughter. You couldn't ask for two better guys to be the voice of this book—experts both in skills and storytelling. But perhaps what they do best is capturing all the fun to be had in the outdoors, from the big-game woods to a humble farm pond. Every page of this book is designed to help you enjoy every second you spend outside.

As for my own redneck status, the big city where I live and work doesn't always present the best opportunities to get out and go wild. Still, that hasn't kept me from escaping when I can and adding my own experiences to the redneck code.

You might be a redneck if you've drunk cheap whiskey around a campfire . . .

You might be a redneck if you've had the blood of a wild hog you killed smeared on your face . . .

You might be a redneck if you preserved the tail of the first squirrel you shot to use as a bookmark . . .

You might be a redneck if you've ridden the subway carrying a fresh black-bear hide inside a cooler . . .

You might be a redneck if you're dying to see what fun awaits in this book . . .

Hell yes I am.

Who's with me?

— COLIN KEARNS
Editor-in-Chief, *Field & Stream*

WHAT IS A REDNECK?

There's been plenty of ink spilled about this creature, the redneck. Some of it funny, much of it stupid, and just about all of it wrong. We're both routinely asked: "Aren't you offended when someone calls you a redneck?" Lately, we've gotten: "Will you have to schedule an apology tour once the book is published?"

The answer to both questions is "no." We aren't planning any apologies because we know what real rednecks are—male or female, knee-high or codger. Succinctly describing a redneck is admittedly difficult, but you know one when you meet one.

He's the old man who can dig a lifeless outboard motor out of a junk pile and have it running in a few hours. Or the guy who can sight in his .22 with two shots, then go shoot a limit of squirrels—each behind the shoulder because the brains are the second-best part after the saddle. She's the gal who figured out how to hook the disc to the tractor because no way in this world was she going to ask for help. Rednecks believe that a sucker, freshly gigged out of a cold Ozark stream, is the tastiest fish there is, and that a titty is the best way to quantify the size of a bream.

The redneck is not a southern guy or a mountain gal. She might not have finished the sixth grade—but then again, she might have a doctorate. He's the guy who can do things outdoors—hunting, fishing, fixing—that other people cannot. Partly, it's because of experience, skill, and confidence. But it also has a lot to do with upbringing—redneck mamas raise few fools. Mostly, though, it's because rednecks like to tinker and fuss and piddle with stuff that helps them enjoy life out in the woods and creeks and catfish lakes.

That's the thinking behind this book. We want to help folks drop a cricket down deep where the redbellies sulk, to get the perfect grip on a giant flathead catfish, or to put a .22 round up there high where that bushytail has flattened himself on the sycamore limb and is smirking at the squirrel dogs yapping up the trunk. And we want to celebrate all our redneck friends who already do those things.

You'll see that there's a pretty simple structure to this book, because a redneck looks at life head-on. There's hunting. There's fishing. And other than that, there's everything else.

— WILL BRANTLEY &
T. EDWARD NICKENS

HUNTING

My guide's name was Devin Huggard-McInnis, and he was the only one in moose camp who could get to where we were planning to hunt. An unexpected November warm-up had melted the previous week's snow, and the trail's hardpan–if there was one–was beneath at least two feet of mud.

"I've got a Jeep with a winch and big tires. Them others can't get their pickups out here," he said as we slipped along the trail at sunrise, watching the shoulder for moose tracks. "I grew up out here. Trapping. Shooting grouse. Playing in the mud."

"Out here" is the bleak and beautiful country of northwestern Alberta—2,200 miles from my home turf of Western Kentucky—a place where wolves and grizzly bears live, and where guys like Devin say things like "ki-yoot."

"You mean coyote?" I asked him. We were discussing his substantial trap line, of which the other guides in camp seemed envious.

"Yeah, ki-yoots. That's what I said."

Late the next day, with the quarters, skull, and antlers of a 42-inch bull moose tucked behind the back seat, we buried Devin's Jeep in enough mud that steam began billowing from under the hood. "She's a little hot," he said as he put it in park.

We were 30 miles from the nearest house and probably not much less from the nearest vehicle. We fished a couple water bottles that had been upcycled as tobacco spitters from the floorboards and sliced the necks off them. After breaking through skim ice in trailside puddles, we filled the bottles with cold, tannic water and began cleaning the grill and drenching the engine the best we could. The methane-heavy steam produced by the heated puddle water smelled the same as it would have if we'd been hung up in a mud hole in south Georgia. Devin worked with a cigarette hanging from his lips.

"You take any offense to being called a redneck, Devin?" I asked.

"Hell, no. Up here, that's like a badge of pride, eh?" He slammed the hood of his Jeep and started it up.

"That's kind of what I thought," I said.

That night in camp we had a moose to celebrate and some beers to drink. And something I've known for years was confirmed once again: Hunt camps full of rednecks are universally good places to be. —W.B.

SMALL GAME

This is where it all started for so many of us. Hotfooting after rabbits. Chasing after squirrels. The brushpile kicking in hopes of stirring up a pheasant or quail. Hunting small game is how we honed our craft—learned to shoot, track, and drift through the woods like smoke.

It's a crying shame that so many folks think of small-game hunting as nothing more than kid stuff. All those hunts that were such fun in our youth are just as fun today—and you don't need to carry a treestand on your back to do any of them.

Hopefully the tips, techniques, and dirty tricks that follow will get you back out in the field—or keep you there—chasing all those pocket-size critters that can produce some awfully big memories. After all, there's nothing small about the pride that comes from cooking up a squirrely pot of Brunswick stew. —T.E.N.

001 KNOW YOUR SQUIRREL DOGS

Along with a flintlock and black iron pans, a treeing dog was an essential part of the pioneer's kit. A dog that could herd a milk cow, bay a hog, and tree a squirrel was as necessary as a hoe or adze. Various lines of curs and feists have spread across Redneck America. In squirrel season they still get it done. Here are some of the most well known.

TREEING FEIST Weighing less than 30 pounds, these small dogs are easy to handle, and you can fit more than one in a dog box. Feists tend to hunt close and use their eyes more than a cur, and they'll timber the squirrel a little quicker. Many hunt quietly, making it easy to hear what other hunters are saying and where they're moving.

MOUNTAIN CUR A mountain cur works a bit like a Treeing Walker Coonhound or a pocket-size bloodhound—climbing fallen trees, poking a snout into every knothole, burrowing into thickets. They tend to range farther than feists and to run a track by scent. When they tree, they're up on the trunk, staying tight and barking plenty, like a hound.

BLACKMOUTH CUR These are larger dogs, from 40 to 90 pounds, and they almost always have a black mask around a squarish muzzle, with the black color extending onto the gums and roof of the mouth. The Black Mouth Cur has amazing winding ability. It'll walk on its two hind legs, like a kangaroo, with its nose in the air trying to smell a squirrel.

002 CALL SQUIRRELS WITH STUFF IN YOUR JUNK DRAWER

In his historic 1984 research paper on squirrel vocabulary, Dr. Robert Lishak identified four different alarm vocalizations—the *buzz*, *kuk*, *quaa*, and *moan*. But squirrels have cussed me out using no fewer than 83 potty-mouthed slurs, so four strikes me as a bit low.

There are lots of squirrel calls on the market, but no one in their right mind would shell out hard-earned money when these three junk-drawer objects will do the trick.

TOY SQUEAKER The small plastic bulb inside a squeaky dog toy can imitate the distress call of a young squirrel. That racket, in turn, draws other squirrels that are concerned or just plain curious. Use the toy squeaker early in the season, when young squirrels are still plentiful.

BOLT AND WASHER Cutter calls involve a ridged rod and a striker, and replicate the sound of a squirrel

working on a tough nut. For the rod, try threaded plastic bolts, metal bolts, or even the brass bolts that hold toilet seats in place. Cutter calls are killer after you've been busted. Sit quietly for 10 minutes, then lure the squirrel back into the open.

SPARE CHANGE The clink-clank of a couple coins can turn a squirrel inside out with curiosity. Rub the ridged edges of two quarters together to make a nut-cutting sound. Poker chips are even louder. Or hold a quarter and a penny between your thumb and forefinger and rasp them together in short, quick movements. The sound is amazingly similar to a squirrel going hog wild on a hickory nut.
—T.E.N.

003 BARK A SQUIRREL

It's true: Redneck wannabe John James Audubon once saw Daniel Boone—America's first and original redneck—"bark" a squirrel in ol' Kaintuck, and, soon after, every pioneer in the backcountry was trying to knock tree rats senseless. The idea is simple: A .50-caliber slug would pulverize a squirrel, so by striking the tree branch just below the critter's noggin, the bark and branch shrapnel half-brains the squirrel, and keeps it fit for the pot. Barking a squirrel became the mark of a sharpshooter, and still is. Here's how to do it.

USE ENOUGH GUN A .22 will likely not provide enough concussive power, so try barking squirrels with a deer gun. To really test your mettle against the frontiersmen, go with a .32-caliber blackpowder rifle.

DELIVER SOME CHIN MUSIC Aim at the tree branch directly under the squirrel's head. Try to place the bullet so that it hits the branch above its centerline. That way, it will splinter the branch rather than become embedded in the wood.

HUSTLE UP Be ready to hoof it to the tree to fully dispatch your dazed squirrel. A pocketknife will do the trick.

004 MAKE A SQUIRREL TOTE

From a simple wire coat hanger, you can make a couple of game totes that will work for squirrels and rabbits alike. Here's how.

STEP 1 Using needle-nose pliers with cutters, snip the hanger about 6 inches from either bend on both the top and bottom sides of the hanger (you'll now have the makings for two totes).

STEP 2 The bottom will be straight wire, and you'll want to leave it as such. Bend the end of the top wire into an inch-long open loop, so that you can hook it around the bottom wire.

STEP 3 Using a small mill-bastard (I love that word) file, sharpen the straight end to a point.

STEP 4 When you kill a squirrel, open the tote, run the point through the skin between the tendons and bones of the rear legs, and then hook the tote shut.

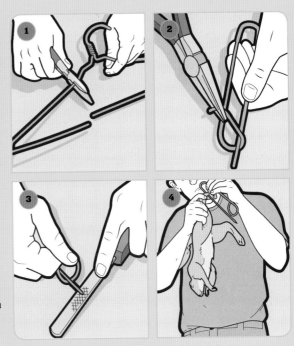

005 PIMP YOUR .22

A dear uncle gave me my first gun, a J.C. Higgins Model 31 tube-fed .22 he bought at Sears. I shot it for years, but one .22 is never enough. Right now, my current rimfire love is the equivalent of a trophy wife with a loyalty card at the plastic surgeon's office: a Ruger 10/22 pimped to the max. Still, it's not so showy that you'd feel stupid unsheathing it at your granddaddy's farm. —T.E.N.

DROP-IN TRIGGER Replacing the 10/22's famously unimpressive factory trigger is a snap. Timney's one-piece, aircraft-grade aluminum drop-in trigger is set at a crisp 2¾ pounds with no creep.

LAMINATED STOCK With grain in their multiple layers of wood running in different directions, laminated stocks offer high strength and resistance to warping.

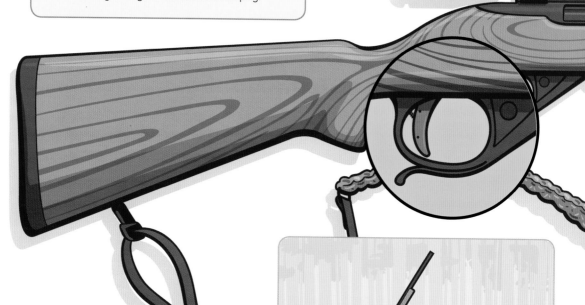

006 GO PRONE FOR TREE TOPPERS

When I hunted with Mac English, the patriarch of South Carolina squirrel dogging, he was 77 years old and still going strong. English and his brother developed a funky shooting stance that enabled them to smack squirrels from the tippy-tops of big oaks when there were no other trees to serve as a rifle rest. In English's unorthodox prone position, your upper arm and entire upper body are in solid contact with the ground, bolstered by a bent leg that serves as an outrigger.

STEP 1 With your rifle in your left hand, lie on your right side. Keep your right thigh in a straight line with your torso, and bend your right knee so that your right foot points back at 90 degrees.

STEP 2 Cross your left leg over the right, placing your left foot just above the right knee joint or across the right knee and on the ground. Put the rifle to your shoulder, keeping the upper right arm on the ground. Hold the fore-end in your left hand; keep that hand firmly on your left knee.

STEP 3 Make minor adjustments by shifting the left knee slightly, keeping solid contact between the left leg and the right knee joint (or ground) at all times. —T.E.N.

DEDICATED RIMFIRE SCOPE The 50-yard parallax setting on the Nikon Prostaff 3–9x40 BDC 150 gives a squirrel hunter tack-sharp focus, while the BDC reticle is calibrated for .22 Long Rifle ammo.

VOLQUARTSEN CARBON FIBER BARREL At a short 16 ½ inches, and just 23 ounces in weight, the carbon fiber barrel shroud is put together with tension at both the muzzle and chamber ends. For long walks in the woods, it's the squirrel's pajamas.

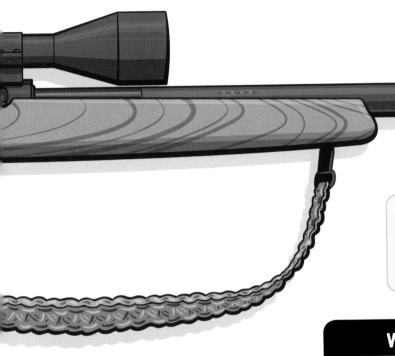

PARACORD SLING Sandstorm Custom Rifle Slings weaves some of the best paracord slings around. Mine is in a standard weave for a supple feel, but the double cobra and king cobra designs are pretty sweet, too.

007 EAT SQUIRREL BRAINS

Squirrel brains are a Southern delicacy. After skinning your squirrels, simply cut off the heads, pluck out the eyeballs, and fry the heads whole in a skillet. Then, use a fork to flip open the skullcap like the lid of a Zippo lighter. The brain is white, about the size of a pecan, and has a mild flavor—you know, like most any brain.

The New York Times once put out a report linking squirrel-brain breakfasts to Creutzfeldt-Jakob disease—a type of encephalopathy. The research was conducted by a Kentucky doctor and documented in a dozen or so cases, but dismissed by most ardent brain eaters I know. Far more people, they claimed, have gone crazy living in New York City. —w.b.

WHAT THE #*&! IS A
WARBLE

It's the nastiest thing on God's green Earth: a fingernail-size, goo-oozing lesion sometimes found on the skin of an early-season squirrel. Each one is filled with the black grublike larvae of a botfly, and squirrels can be so lumped up that they look like a gray bag of marbles. The larvae hatch in late summer, and the gross boils are largely healed by the first frost. These so-called "warbles" or "wolves" are skin parasites only and don't affect the meat—although you'd have to be one tough customer to stew up such a lumpy squirrel.

008

SELL A LITTLE TAIL FOR POCKET MONEY

You probably won't be able to buy mama a new truck by selling squirrel tails to Mepps, but the lure company does pay hard cash for high-quality tails, which it uses to manufacture some of the best-selling in-line spinners on the planet. No joke. Mepps buys tens of thousands of squirrel tails each year from hunters and entrepreneurial roadkill pickers. Expect to earn between 16¢ and 26¢ per tail. Or, if you're filthy rich and don't need the extra scratch, Mepps will double your money in trade-in value for new lures. Yet another reason why America is the greatest country on Earth.

HELL, I CAN SKIN THAT!

SQUIRRELS

Ounce for ounce, there is no North American critter tougher to skin than a big squirrel. The size of a mature boar's tackle is indicative of the task ahead. The bigger they are, the tougher he'll be. A squirrel's skin is thick, tough, and covered in fur that seems to be magnetically drawn to squirrel meat. But, with the correct technique, you can remove a squirrel's hide in less than a minute while keeping the meat clean and sweet. Here's how.

BREAK THE TAIL Cut around the base of the tailbone, just above the butthole (rednecks don't say "anus"). Twist and break the tailbone, but leave it attached to the hide.

MAKE GUIDE CUTS With your knife's edge turned upward, make a one-inch incision from the tail along the top of each hind leg. Skin this section away from the squirrel until you have a flap large enough to stand on with your boot.

PUT YOUR FOOT DOWN Lay the squirrel top side down on a piece of wood (or any clean, flat surface) and place your boot on that skin flap, using the squirrel's tailbone to keep it from slipping. Grab both hind legs at the ankles and slowly but deliberately pull the carcass away from the hide. The skin should easily peel off over the head and front legs.

GET TO THE POINT Done right, you'll be left with skin on the back legs that extends to a point on the belly. While holding the squirrel under the shoulders with one hand, grab that point with the other hand and pull. Your newly hide-less squirrel is now ready to gut or quarter for the frying pan.

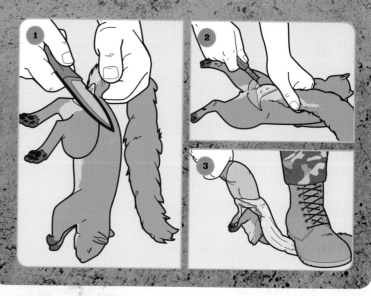

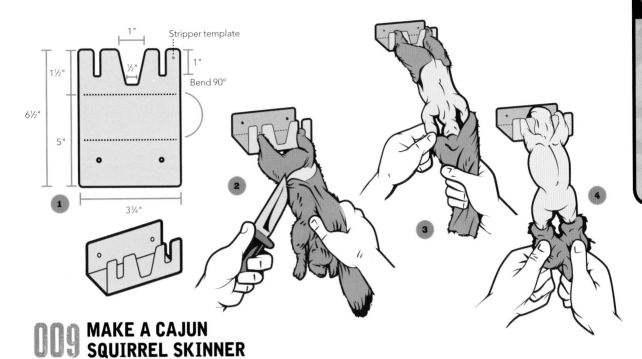

009 MAKE A CAJUN SQUIRREL SKINNER

Once you become a squirrel-killing machine and the critters start piling up, you might find that you want a more efficient way to process them. I witnessed this little trick device help my Cajun pals clean a washtub full of squirrels in no time flat.

STEP 1 The first step is to make the skinner, using the template shown here to cut and bend a 6 ½x3 ¾-inch piece of ¹⁄₁₆-inch aluminum plate. Nail the squirrel skinner to a tree or post at shoulder height. Now you're ready to rumble. Hook the squirrel's rear legs in the two narrow slots with its back facing you.

STEP 2 Bend the tail over the squirrel's back and make a cut between the butthole and the base of the tail, through the skin and tailbone. Extend this cut about an inch down the backbone and then down each side of the squirrel another inch, just in front of the thighs.

STEP 3 Next, grasp the tail and loosened hide, and pull down. The hide should shuck off inside out, except for a strip on the belly and the back legs.

STEP 4 Flip the squirrel over and place its neck in the wide slot and its front paws in the two narrow slots. Grasp the remaining hide and strip the "pants" off the squirrel. —T.E.N.

010 PRESERVE A SQUIRREL TAIL

Be honest: Who *wouldn't* want an awesome squirrel tail hanging from their rearview mirror? Just make sure you do it this way, because nobody wants a skanky squirrel tail stinking up their ride.

Make a slit at the base of the tail, grasp the bone with pliers or a paper towel, and very gently pull and push the furry part of the tail off the bone. Scrape away as much fat and meat as you can reach, then sprinkle 20 Mule Team borax on the flesh. Insert a straw into the tail and pour in as much borax as possible. Insert a thin wire, stitch up the opening, and hang it in a cool, dry place for a week or two.

011

TAKE A BUNNY STAND

Sometimes the cartoons are right—a wascally wabbit may not sing opera, but it really will run in circles. That means that its habit of looping back to the very patch of ground where it was jumped is the chink in its armor. When the dogs jump a bunny, find a good place to take a stand, but know that its return could take anywhere from five minutes to half an hour. But don't wait on the dogs—the rabbit could return well in front of the pack. Here are a few additional tips.

HOG THE ROAD Logging and farm roads are a perfect ambush. The trick: Put your back to the brush so you're looking across the road and into the woods where the rabbit is running. Often, you'll see it tiptoe to the edge before making the final dash.

PATROL THE BORDER Bunnies often squirt out of the thick stuff for a short burst of speed, so post up on open edges between fields and woods.

TAKE A KNEE Deep-woods cottontails like to find the occasional opening where they can turn on the afterburners. Get down on one knee in a stretch of open timber. You'll be able to see the rabbit coming and still swing on the animal as it passes.

WATCH THE EDGE Interior woods edges between pine thickets and more open hardwoods are great spots to snipe rabbits dashing out of cover.

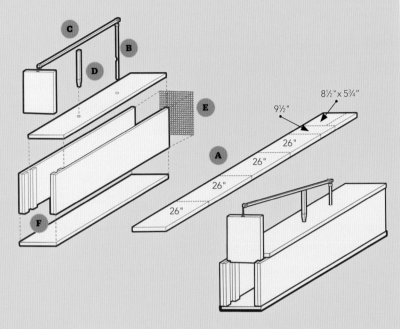

012 BUILD A RABBIT GUM

For the last hundred years, any country bumpkin worth his snuff has run a line of rabbit gums to keep the family in fried bunny. Early settlers used fire to hollow out black gum logs for their bunny traps, hence the name, but rabbit gums today are made of plank wood or old barn siding. If you've never built one, get to it—or hand in your redneck card.

STEP 1 Saw a 10-foot 1x8 plank (A) as shown.

STEP 2 Craft the trigger (B) as shown with a ½-inch wooden dowel cut to 11 inches; the door lever (C) a piece ¾ inches wide and 18 ½ inches long; and a fulcrum post (D) ¾ inches wide and 6 ¾ inches long.

STEP 3 Traditional gums had a solid back panel; make yours from see-through hardware cloth or chicken wire (E) because ol' wabbit will feel better when he can see all the way through the trap before entering. Plus, you'll be able to see what you caught before opening the door on a pissed-off 'possum.

STEP 4 Make four door guides (F) from ¾ x ¾-inch wood cut to the same height as the sides of the box. Assemble the trap with nails or wood screws. The door should slide freely between the guides. Cut a ½-inch-deep notch into the trigger to hold it in place, leaving 5 inches extending into the trap. Use string to tie the door and the trigger to the lever.

STEP 5 Leave your unbaited gum along a rabbit run in thick cover for a week to allow critters to get used to it. After that, set your bait between the trigger stick and the back panel. Use aromatic goodies such as apples. Old-timers used cabbage, turnips, salt, and carrots, of course. It's not a bad idea to create a Hansel-and-Gretel trail of small bait pieces that lead to the trap's entrance, and crush a piece of bait and smear it around the inside of the gum to lead the rabbit to the point of no return.

013 HANG A SWAMP RABBIT

Part alligator, part merganser, a swamp rabbit is a different breed of bunny altogether. They're at least twice the size of a cottontail, with more wits than a coyote and more speed than a fox. And they're as happy swimming a swamp as tunneling through briars. The first time I reached down to snatch a dead swamp rabbit from an Alabama beaver slough, 15 fleas hopped onto my bare hand. I jumped back like I'd stepped on a cottonmouth. Shooting swamp bucks in front of yodeling beagles is whopper fun, but these Southern hares can be slam covered up with fleas.

To rid a bunny of bugs, hang it from a low branch for a couple hours right after you shoot it. Remember the spot, or mark it on a GPS. Blood-sucking varmints will flee the cooling carcass, and you'll be able to pick it up later without having to worry about becoming patient zero for the next strain of bubonic plague. That said, it's not a bad idea to keep your hunting vest in the bed of the truck, and then hang it outside when you get back home. —T.E.N

014 SPEAK LIKE A HOUNDSMAN

It's the redneck's hound-dog mantra: When the tailgate drops, the B.S. stops. So you better know the houndsman's vocabulary to understand just what's going on in that bunny thicket or coon holler. Here's a glossary to help sort out the foreign language.

JUMP DOG A dog known for its ability to find and jump game animals and make them run. Also called a "strike dog."

TRACK DOG These dogs are single-minded and persistent—when the scent trail goes cold, they stay the course, working the track close to figure out where the animal ran. Also called a "trail dog" or "picker."

SWING DOG When the pack loses the trail, these dogs range back and forth in an attempt to pick up the track. A good pack will have both track dogs and swing dogs.

LINE CONTROL The ability of a dog to stay close to the scent trail.

TONGUE The special voice of a hound on scent. A dog's tongue will change as conditions change on the trail.

CHOP MOUTH A short, choppy, staccato style of tonguing, also called "machine gun." Opposite of "bawl mouth," characterized by a big, booming tongue.

TIGHT MOUTH Describes a dog that only tongues when on scent. Also, "clean mouth." But sometimes used for a dog that doesn't tongue sufficiently when on trail.

BABBLING When a hound tongues or "opens up" indiscriminately.

GONE TO GROUND A critter that disappears into a hole or burrow has "gone to ground."

CHECK When the dogs lose the scent trail. Also used to describe a change of course or tactics employed by the rabbit.

TAILING Describes dogs that look at their pack-mates to see what they are doing, instead of hunting on their own.

015 HUNT A JUNKYARD

The best rabbit spot I've ever seen was a clandestine scrapyard near an old railroad bed on the edge of town. Though I doubt anyone ever paid a dumping fee for using the place, there were years' worth of abandoned cars, boats, appliances, lumber, tin, and other assorted tetanus-causing junk scattered alongside the tracks. It was all grown over with blackberry vines and brambles, and it was absolutely full of rabbits.

My former college roommate Ryan is a beagle man, and he believes the mark of a good dog is one that will burrow into such a place and spend plenty of time nosing around. "Lots of rabbits are missed in places like this, because a dog won't get down in the trash to really look for them," he says. Over his dogs, we killed the fire out of rabbits in that junkyard.

Even jump-shooters can have good luck in a place like that if they follow the same advice—you just have to plow through the thickest stuff you can see. Pausing frequently as you walk makes bunnies nervous and prone to bolting out of cover, be it a strip of native grasses or the crumpled hood of an old Buick. —W.B.

HELL, I CAN SKIN THAT!

RABBITS

Were we to establish a scale of critter-cleaning difficulty, rabbits would be near the bottom. Here's how to ready a rabbit for the table.

STEP 1 Grab the rabbit under the front shoulders with one hand, and squeeze the ribcage with the other while working your hand down toward the hind legs. The guts will pop right out the rear end.

STEP 2 Near a hind ankle, pinch up a bit of fur and skin, twist it slightly, and pull downward, peeling away a strip of skin. Grasp the remaining hide and carefully peel it off the rabbit. Often, the hide will come loose in two or three sections, and you'll be left with skin on the legs, head, and tail.

STEP 3 Cut off the feet, head, and tailbone. Open the chest cavity, and rinse away any remaining guts and blood with cold water. The rabbit's now ready to be cooked whole or quartered, depending on your supper of choice. With practice, you should be able to clean a good-size cottontail in about a minute.

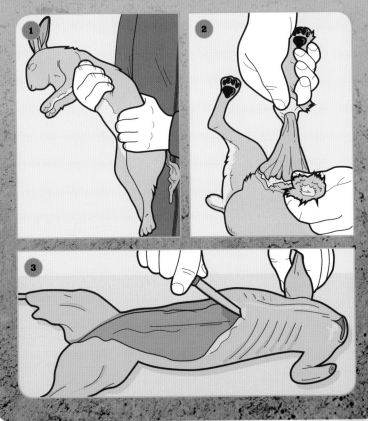

016

TOTE A SINGLE SHOT

Whatever I'm hunting, whether it's doves or geese or gobblers, I tend to use a 12-gauge semiauto most of the year. But there's no real urgency to a rabbit hunt, so when I'm out chasing down bunnies, I enjoy carrying a single-shot shotgun with me that otherwise sees little use. A single-shot is light and a joy to carry all day; besides that, it's just a quintessential redneck weapon. My sentimental favorite is the 16-gauge Model 37 Winchester that my dad gave to me many years ago. But if I were shopping for a new single-shot rabbit gun, I'd go with an H&R Topper in 20 gauge. Having only one shot will cost you a bunny from time to time, but that's rarely a problem in this particular game. It just means that the chase goes on a little longer.
—W.B.

BLOCK OUT FOR BUSHYTAILS

When I hunted withMac English, he was 77 years old, lean and wiry, with a head of white hair that was easier to follow through the South Carolina hardwoods than the man himself. A major player in the comeback of the Original Mountain Cur, a famed squirrel dog breed, English was still hunting six days a week. And hunting hard. One year, his hunting parties treed and shot a staggering 544 gray squirrels.

I'd been advised to bring my A-game. "Mac English has an extreme, over-the-top pride in shooting squirrels in the head," Jim LaPratt explained to me on the phone a few weeks prior to my hunt. A die-hard Michigan squirrel dogger himself, LaPratt runs the website Squirrel Dog Central (sqdog.com), the virtual Bible of the sport. "He's turned head shots into an art form."

To English, the only sin more unforgivable than missing a squirrel's noggin is ruining its flavorful meat. The first time we step out of the truck, he warns me: "Boy, you shoot a squirrel and there ain't no need to run up there and jerk him off the ground and put him in your vest where nobody can see him. We got to inspect him, and I'll raise sand if there's a hole anywhere but the head."

My first shot on a squirrel, early in the hunt, brings down a heap of scorn from English.

"Oh, Lord," he says, holding my squirrel with two fingers like a soiled diaper. It is a picture-perfect gall bladder shot, with bits of red guts pushed out the far side of the ribs. "Oh, goodness. Somebody else is going to have to carry this thing. Looking at it just about makes me sick."

Now I'm on the verge of sinning big time. Four grown men, two kids, three dogs, five guns, and thousands of dollars' worth of high-tech optics and GPS dog collars surround a squirrel in a tree. It's my turn to shoot and, thank my lucky stars, the squirrel is stretched out on a sunny branch like a college kid at Daytona Beach.

English never makes it easy. He's at my elbow, pouring it on.

"It just don't seem right," he says, "that squirrel sitting out there in the open. Really, you ought to be ashamed taking a shot like that."

The crosshairs waver for a moment as English keeps up the pressure, 24 inches from my right ear. "My goodness, you ought to have some mercy on that poor little squirrel, all stretched out in the sunshine."

I let out half a breath and begin to squeeze.

"Oh, Lord, look at the squirrel. Glad it ain't my shot. No excuses now."

I pull the trigger and the squirrel tumbles. The dogs are barking and my buddies are whooping and Mr. Mac is hoofing it to the tree. It's a small squirrel, a yearling as tender as a green bean, and already English can taste it. "That's a fryer, boys! Get the dogs! I don't want a tooth on him!"

—T.E.N.

017 KNOW YOUR HOUNDS

You've got a dog, and you've got a truck—right? Let's see if we can accurately match up your hound to your lifestyle.

YOUR DOG	YOU ARE . . .	YOUR RIG
BLUETICK COONHOUND 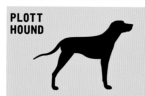 The spotted, splotched country companion of coon hunters from sea to shining sea.	Single (or soon to be). How else can you spend five nights a week chasing ringtails?	Full-size Ford Bronco—not that sissy Bronco II—with used 33-inch mudders that you traded for your ratty old Honda three-wheeler on Craigslist.
PLOTT HOUND A rangy beast of a dog, originally bred by mountain men in North Carolina to run bear and boar.	Pulling down serious cash as an oil-rig roughneck, which is how you can afford to run bears with the baddest big-game dog on the planet.	Early-'70s Chevy with the long bed, three on the tree, and the requisite Calvin-peeing-on-Ford cab sticker.
BEAGLE  The happy-go-lucky everyman's hound that will sleep on your couch for 10 months of the year and run rabbits like a fiend the other two.	Juggling youth-league baseball games with your bunny hunts. Nothing says "family man" like a pack of beagles.	F-150, with two toddler seats in the back you borrowed from your cousin to save a few bucks. And a $1,500 dog box in the bed, which you told your wife was on blowout for $250.
ORIGINAL MOUNTAIN CUR*  A dog that nearly vanished from history until being bred back to glory by four forward-thinking bluegrass musicians in the 1950s.	Watching *Swamp People* reruns and running your hand through a luxurious mullet. The hardest-working squirrel dog in the hardwoods deserves a serious redneck, after all.	El Camino—it's the mullet of vehicles: Business up front, party in the back.
BLACK MOUTH CUR* The breed made famous by *Old Yeller*. Sweet as dandelion wine—unless you're a squirrel and it's hungry.	Tracking cow manure through the living room. Black Mouth Curs are part herding dog, part hog killer—not exactly for sensitive types.	Chevy S-10—every redneck needs a truck, but not every redneck can afford a whole one.
BASSET HOUND  A lovable beast, though very few retain the hunting instincts of their ancestors.	Hiding a copy of *Wine Spectator* under a *Field & Stream* from 1998.	Subaru Outback—but your other car is a Prius.
CATAHOULA LEOPARD DOG* A striking cur with "cracked glass" blue eyes. Legend has it the line reaches back to red wolves domesticated by the Indians.	A Cajun, a wannabe Cajun, or a frat boy who heard these dogs are cool. They are cool—if you run wild hogs for fun.	Jeep Comanche, with a set of real truck nuts hanging from the hitch, not the stupid plastic ones you buy on the Internet.

*Save your breath. Even curs wish they were hounds.

BIG GAME

How do you define "big game"? Many of us start with deer—and whitetails in particular. Since deer hunting is so deeply ingrained in the typical *Field & Stream* reader's outdoor experience—and indeed in redneck culture in general—we tend to talk and write about it independently from elk, moose, bears, and the like.

Yet, even if you never do anything but hunt whitetails in your home county, you're a big-game hunter as far as we're concerned. If properly rationed, even a yearling doe will provide a month's worth of suppers. To us, that qualifies as big game.

Of course, like the moose we mentioned at the start of this chapter, North American big game critters get a lot bigger than your standard whitetail. We don't have room in this book to go in-depth on all of them, but we managed to provide insight on each of our favorites. —W.B

018 HUNT A 20-ACRE WOODS

Whether you're trying to kill enough deer for the annual Baptist church venison feed or tag a big buck, consistent success on whitetails comes from a delicate balance of two variables: persistence and pressure management. You'll never kill a buck from the couch (unless your couch is in a tree), but you probably won't kill him if you hunt him too much, either.

For most of the year, a whitetail's home range is about 600 acres; a big buck's core area can be as little as 50 acres. That's why I'll take three good 20-acre farms over one okay 100-acre farm every time. But the small farms have to be hunted carefully.

SCOUT IT Learning whether deer use the tract as a bedding or feeding area is the first step in deciding how to hunt it. In general, hunt food in the evenings and cover in mornings.

USE STEALTH There's nothing on 20 acres you can't walk to, so learn how to access your stands undetected. That means staying hidden from deers' eyes and their noses. I can get to one of my best north-wind stands in about five minutes by walking in from the main pull-off—but my scent will blow right into a bedding thicket on the way in. Instead, I circle around the farm, walk down a blacktop road, and then sneak up a deep ravine to my stand. It's an extra 20 minutes of walking, but it's worth every step.

STRIKE WHILE IT'S HOT Don't mistake "pressure management" for not hunting at all. If you're seeing deer and not spooking them—especially during the rut—stay put. Food sources and patterns change, so you have to be in the tree at the best times. —W.B.

WHAT THE %$#^IS A

HOLLER

A holler is the southern Appalachian version of the word "hollow." Some say the word "holler" comes from a narrow creek bottom between two wooded ridges. Others say that a man could stand on one end and hear his buddy yell—or holler—from the other.

Either way, a holler funnels movement of deer, turkeys, and all sorts of game, and frequently provides edge cover between upland and bottomland habitat types, making it an excellent place to hunt.

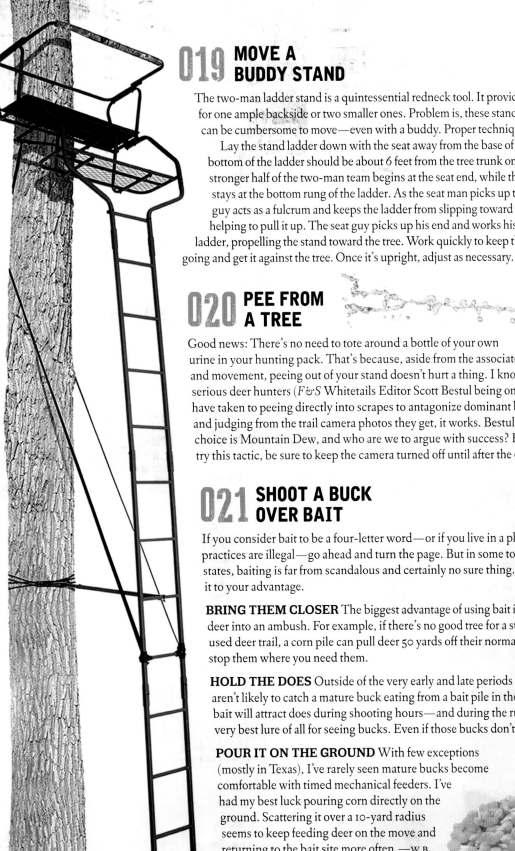

019 MOVE A BUDDY STAND

The two-man ladder stand is a quintessential redneck tool. It provides enough room for one ample backside or two smaller ones. Problem is, these stands are heavy and can be cumbersome to move—even with a buddy. Proper technique is essential.

Lay the stand ladder down with the seat away from the base of the tree. The bottom of the ladder should be about 6 feet from the tree trunk on flat ground. The stronger half of the two-man team begins at the seat end, while the other person stays at the bottom rung of the ladder. As the seat man picks up the stand, the other guy acts as a fulcrum and keeps the ladder from slipping toward the tree, while also helping to pull it up. The seat guy picks up his end and works his way down the ladder, propelling the stand toward the tree. Work quickly to keep the momentum going and get it against the tree. Once it's upright, adjust as necessary.

020 PEE FROM A TREE

Good news: There's no need to tote around a bottle of your own urine in your hunting pack. That's because, aside from the associated noise and movement, peeing out of your stand doesn't hurt a thing. I know several serious deer hunters (*F&S* Whitetails Editor Scott Bestul being one) who have taken to peeing directly into scrapes to antagonize dominant bucks— and judging from the trail camera photos they get, it works. Bestul's beverage of choice is Mountain Dew, and who are we to argue with success? However, if you try this tactic, be sure to keep the camera turned off until after the deed is done.

021 SHOOT A BUCK OVER BAIT

If you consider bait to be a four-letter word—or if you live in a place where such practices are illegal—go ahead and turn the page. But in some top-tier whitetail states, baiting is far from scandalous and certainly no sure thing. Here's how to use it to your advantage.

BRING THEM CLOSER The biggest advantage of using bait is that it can lure a deer into an ambush. For example, if there's no good tree for a stand near a well-used deer trail, a corn pile can pull deer 50 yards off their normal travel route and stop them where you need them.

HOLD THE DOES Outside of the very early and late periods of the season, you aren't likely to catch a mature buck eating from a bait pile in the daylight. But bait will attract does during shooting hours—and during the rut, does are the very best lure of all for seeing bucks. Even if those bucks don't come to the corn.

POUR IT ON THE GROUND With few exceptions (mostly in Texas), I've rarely seen mature bucks become comfortable with timed mechanical feeders. I've had my best luck pouring corn directly on the ground. Scattering it over a 10-yard radius seems to keep feeding deer on the move and returning to the bait site more often. —w.b.

022 GRAB A BUCK BY THE OYSTERS

You can remove the oysters (also known as inner loins or tenderloins) from a deer without having to gut it first—which is handy if you ever need to quarter a buck and haul him home one piece at a time. First, you'll need to skin the deer. Then, cut a shallow incision along the spine, from the deer's last rib back to the edge of the hip. Reach through that hole, and feel along the underside of the spine. On a good-size buck, the loin will be about the diameter of your wrist. Use your knife to carefully cut away the front end of the loin, and you should then be able to gently pull it right out of the deer. Cool the meat quickly, and repeat on the other side.

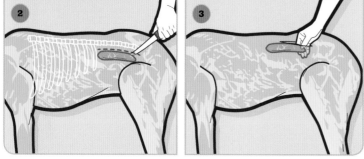

024

FIX YOUR BOW WITH DENTAL FLOSS

Even if you never use it to clean your teeth, a spool of dental floss is invaluable in an archery repair kit. The high-stress areas of your bow's strings and cables—such as the arrow nocking point—are wrapped with an extra layer of protection called serving. Bow shops use special serving material, but if you notice serving wear in the field, 10 inches of dental floss and a drop of superglue should mend it well enough for you to keep hunting for about a week. It's also handy for securing peep sights and kisser buttons. Think of it as bowhunter's duct tape.

023 MAKE RATTLING ANTLERS

You can always buy a plastic rattling contraption from Walmart—but where's the fun in that? The best rattling antlers come from the rack of a decent-size 10-point whitetail, with tines at least 5 inches long and beams heavy enough to make a resonating *crack* when slammed together. First, remove the brow tines with a hacksaw and file the stumps clean. Next, drill a quarter-inch hole between each brow stump and pedicle, and thread a foot-long piece of paracord through each antler. Tie knots in the ends of the cord, and presto: You're ready to put on a one-man buck fight.

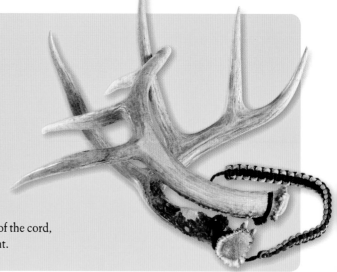

025 KNOW YOUR X-BOW

The crossbow concept might be ancient, but the tricked-out models of today are anything but primitive. Rednecks certainly appreciate crossbows, and the reasons are many. For one, the most famous redneck on television, Daryl Dixon, carries one on *The Walking Dead.* Entertainment aside, the reasons are eminently practical. More and more states are permitting the use of crossbows during archery season, and they have created a huge market for top-end crossbows and accessories. Plus, they're just fun to shoot. It's difficult to fire crossbow arrows—called bolts—with a modern crossbow and not be impressed with its power and accuracy.

What crossbows are not, however, are arrow-shooting rifles—and some hunters run into trouble when they treat them as such. If you hunt with a crossbow, remember these few rules and you'll be just fine.

USE THE GEAR YOU'RE GIVEN Ol' Daryl cocks his crossbow by hand and uses it to shoot sharpened sticks. In reality, that would ruin his bow—and, over time, his hands. Crossbow arrows vary in size and configuration, and you can't shoot just any bolt with any bow. For instance, be mindful of the type of nock your bow requires and only shoot bolts with that particular type. And use a cocking device—the one that comes with your crossbow—to ensure that you fully cock the string every time. Pay careful attention to the gear that comes with your bow, and if you have doubts when buying replacements, ask your pro shop or manufacturer.

KEEP IT CLOSE The ergonomics of a crossbow are similar to that of a firearm, so it's tempting, and quite a lot of fun, to shoot one over an extended range. If you're pounding targets, by all means have at it. But a hunter assumes heavy responsibility when taking aim at a deer. A bolt flies at a fraction of the speed of a bullet, so you'll be wise to keep your field shots inside 50 yards.

WAIT FOR THE ANGLE Regardless of what you hunt with, you should always wait for a good shot, but it's especially important with archery gear—including a crossbow. Killing with an arrow requires the proper angle so that the broadhead can reach the animal's vitals with minimal resistance.

KNOW YOUR SURROUNDINGS Crossbows are typically bulky, and firing them releases an incredible amount of energy through their limbs, strings, cables, and cams. Before pulling the trigger, make certain nothing on the bow will strike a tree limb, shooting rest, ground blind, or hunting buddy.

026 SPIT-TUNE A MUZZLELOADER

There's no sense in wasting your next Booner loogie. A mouthful of spit could be your ticket to a real wall-hanger. Blackpowder rifles often will shoot better with slightly fouled barrels, and a "spit patch" will clean out any excess fouling without scouring the barrel. Simply spit on a clean patch, place it wet side down on the muzzle, and work it to the breech with a cleaning jag. Remove the patch, reload the gun, and knock the spit out of your next target.

027 AGE VENISON IN A COOLER

When the Binkys of the world are still playing beach bocce, us rednecks are killing deer in our flip-flops. Here's how to age whitetails for four or five days when the mosquitoes are still out.

STEP 1 Skin the deer and cut it into pieces: Shoulders, ribcage with backstraps attached, and the pelvic saddle with both hindquarters intact.

STEP 2 Line the bottom of a large cooler with 2-liter soda bottles that have been filled with water and frozen. Crushed and block ice works, too, but be sure to constantly drain the meltwater to keep it off the meat.

STEP 3 Put in the ribcage first, then the double hams. Work the shoulders in around them. Fill remaining space with bottles of ice. Cover the cooler with a few blankets for extra insulation.

028 MAKE A UTILITY TABLE BUTCHER SHOP

Butchering a deer in your basement separates you from all the schmoes who pay Earl to cut up their meat with the same saw he just used to hack the bumper off an '84 Bronco. This DIY butchering table is easy to make, clean, and store.

STEP 1 Start with a sturdy 6-foot-long, polyethylene-topped folding utility table. Drill holes in one right-hand corner (lefties would use the left-hand edge) to accept the mounting bolts from a manual meat grinder.

STEP 2 Raise the table to a comfortable height with sections of 2-inch PVC pipe slipped over each leg.

STEP 3 Spread out a pair of thin, flexible cutting boards in front of you to protect the edges of your knives when cutting.

STEP 4 Line up three large pans or bowls: one for trimmings that will be tossed, one for chunks of meat destined for the grinder, and the other for finished cuts earmarked for the vacuum packer.

STEP 5 Keep a small bowl filled with hot, soapy water for cleaning knives periodically.

STEP 6 When you're done making meat, clean off the table with a 50/50 mix of bleach and water, and then rinse thoroughly with distilled water.

029 SHOOT A DEER IN FRONT OF DOGS

We get it—running deer with dogs is a major headache for stand and still hunters. But connecting on a whitetail deer being pushed by a hound pack is a skill older than the U.S. of A. herself, and a cherished tradition across much of Redneck America. We're not fans of slinging centerfire bullets at deer running flat out across a beanfield, but dropping a buck at 40 yards with 12-gauge buckshot is a thrill and a skill that will help you bag rabbits, squirrels, and other bouncy, boingy critters. If you get an invite to go deer-dogging from a club with plenty of land and a long heritage, load a 12-gauge with oo buck, and do it the way your granddaddy did. (Or maybe your neighbor's cousin's granddaddy.)

Take a stand where you can shoot at deer in more open areas and can monitor the movement of any nearby dogs or dog drivers. Logging roads are great, but be vigilant if there are shooters to either side of you. Set up on the far side of the road from the oncoming deer so your shots will be in front of other hunters. Internal "edges," such as boundaries between pine stands and hardwoods, will help funnel deer, as will ridge gaps and stream crossings.

Stay quiet and still. Even a running deer will hear you chatting with other hunters and veer away. The trick is to intercept deer as they're tiptoeing out of the danger zone and before the dogs are hot on the trail.

At short range, you won't need to lead the shot by much, if at all. And practicing for such a shot can be a heap of fun. Use baling wire to attach a piece of cardboard to the inside of an old tire, and have a buddy roll it down a hill. As always, be aware of what's beyond the tire.

030 DRAG A DOE WITH A STICK

Does don't come with preinstalled tote handles connected to their heads. To easily drag a doe to the truck, first cut a stout, ¾-inch-diameter stick to 18 inches and whittle a point on one end. Make an inch-long slit in the deer's muzzle, just behind the black part of the nose and across the top of the nose bone. Work the knife blade under the cartilage and out the other side. Insert the stick into this slit. Grab your doe drag with both hands behind your back and start walking.

031 MAKE YOUR OWN COVER SCENTS

You have to beat a deer's nose before you can pull the trigger. Here are four ways to be your own scent manufacturer, ranked by difficulty level.

EASIEST Stuff a pillowcase one-third full with green leaves, pine needles, pieces of bark, moss, acorns—even dirt. Tie a knot in the top of the pillowcase. Prior to a hunt, dampen the pillowcase with water and toss it in the clothes dryer with your hunting duds.

EASY Boil a half gallon of acorns and green pine needles in a gallon of water for 30 minutes. Let the mixture cool, mash the nuts and needles, then boil them again in the same water. Let cool, strain through cheesecloth, and pour the liquid into a spray bottle.

NOT SO BAD Remove the tarsal glands from a buck's hind legs by first cutting around the glands, lifting them with rubber-gloved fingers, and then separating the connective tissue under the skin. Place the glands in a short length of pantyhose, and tie a knot in the top. Store in a sealed plastic bag in a freezer or refrigerator.

HARD In a large kettle, boil 5 gallons of pine needles in 6 to 7 gallons of water (prepare in smaller batches if necessary). Pour this mixture into a washing machine set at the lowest load setting. Toss in clean hunting clothes and wash using the presoak cycle. Clean the washing machine by doing a load of old towels in hot, soapy water. You'd better have the house to yourself if you go this far.

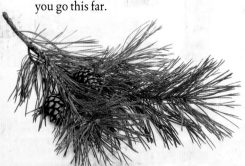

032 PUT ON AN OLD-SCHOOL DEER DRIVE

There are two kinds of deer drives: Those that work, and monkey circuses that end with half the participants pissed off at the other half. The difference comes down to two elements: Command and control.

TAKE COMMAND Elect, appoint, or get out of the way of the group's obvious drive boss, someone who knows the woods inside and out. This person needs to be someone who all the other hunters either respect or fear, and whose instructions they will follow to the letter.

STRIVE FOR CONTROL Drives that end with meat on the ground place a premium on control. That means working small enough tracts of woods to control the movement of deer, in addition to controlling the behaviors of the drivers and standers. Smaller 20- and 30-acre tracts are best—deer tend to slip the noose on larger pieces. Drivers move slowly and in sync. No reason to ring bells or whack pans. Speaking quietly to the other drivers to maintain a straight line will be enough to move deer. Standers should be quiet and still, and never leave their positions until the appointed time. The drive boss will dole out the instructions: when to start, when to stop, and, most important, which directions to never, ever shoot toward.

033 MAKE MEAT

Shoot a meat doe early in the season, every season. Doesn't have to be opening weekend—a good time to put serious horns in the truck—but make meat that first week. It will get the monkey off your back. It will chill out your big-buck jitters. It will stock the camp or family freezer. But mostly, shooting a meat doe will get your mind right: You're in the woods to keep a connection to living off the land, not just to whup your camp pals in blackjack again. Shoot a doe early, and hold your head high when you drag it into camp. If it only takes one hand, well, that's okay, too.

034 LOAD A DEER BY YOURSELF

Getting a deer up and over the tailgate solo is no small task, unless you have two ropes (or a rope and a tow strap) in your truck. And if you don't have at least two ropes in your truck, can you really call yourself a redneck?

STEP 1 Throw one rope over a strong tree branch. Tie one end to a buck's rack or around a doe's neck, and the other to the trailer hitch or tow hooks. Tie a second rope to the deer in the same place—around the antlers or neck—and toss it over the same branch.

STEP 2 Pull the truck forward to lift the deer to the height of your truck bed. Secure the free end of the second rope to the tree trunk at shoulder height, to suspend the deer.

STEP 3 Untie the first rope from the vehicle. Back up, untie the second rope from the tree trunk, and lower the deer into the truck.

035 HUNT A SWAMP BUCK

He's in there, gone deep and hiding because he's tired of the ruckus after a month of rumbling ATVs and slamming truck doors. Big bucks love swamps, from tamarack hellholes in the north to southern buttonbrush and willow sloughs. Yeah, it's hard getting in, and a horror show getting a deer out. That's why you won't see any other hunters in the dark swamp. In other words, he's all yours.

GO DEEP Buy a good pair of hip boots. Hunting pressure in a given spot drops off approximately 99.99 percent when you can't get there in knee boots.

FIND HIGH GROUND Deer don't mind wet feet (I've seen big bucks in Louisiana's Atchafalaya Basin with misshapen hooves due to so much time under water), but they're not amphibious. Look for ridges of high ground, though it doesn't have to be much. Deer will use beaver dams as bridges and bed down on the tops of muskrat huts. The best time to scout for secret swamp passageways is the week after deer season closes. You can stomp around without worrying about busting your next hunt, and deer are still in their hunter-pressured patterns.

HUNT THE LATE SEASON Late in the game, many deer have taken refuge in the gnarliest cover they can find. The good news is that the cold temperatures have knocked back much of the thick stuff. The biggest buck I've killed on my river lease was a late-season buck that was holed up in a cypress swamp. I found a tree overlooking a slough where the winter-dead vegetation had thinned enough for a long shooting lane, and I shot him in the late morning.—T.E.N.

DON'T STEAL YOUR PREGNANT WIFE'S BUCK

On a Friday night, we told my family that Michelle was pregnant. My folks had been asking about a grandchild for eight years. Both of them burst into tears upon hearing the announcement. Mom—a teacher—immediately declared she'd be retiring. My brother, Matt, ran out to his truck and rummaged through the door pocket for a couple celebratory cigars. He returned with grape-flavored Swisher Sweets.

Muzzleloader season opened the next morning, and the jubilant mood at camp was tempered by the reality of hunting in mid-October under a full moon with a woods full of acorns. Matt saw a glimpse of a spike on Saturday afternoon, and that was the extent of the action for the entire day.

Sunday morning was forecast to be cold and clear, so we began making our plans Saturday evening. Dad's plan was to sleep in, and he instructed us to be quiet as we got ready. Matt was going to stick with the stand he'd been hunting in hopes of at least seeing that spike again.

Michelle wanted to hunt the box blind near camp—*her* box blind. It's even labeled as such. On the inside wall, it says, "Mish's Box Blind." Trouble was, we'd hunted Saturday morning and evening, and hadn't seen a deer.

With the woods full of acorns, I told her that the ladder stand up in the timber would be the better bet. It hadn't been hunted all season. I offered to take one for the team and sit the box blind myself. Michelle wasn't crazy about this idea. It would be cold in that ladder stand, and morning sickness is easier to endure inside a box blind. But at my urging, she strapped herself to the tree 30 minutes before daylight, just about the time I was situating myself in the box blind.

The sun rose and began melting the light frost off the food plot in front of me. I heard a few distant shots on the neighboring farms, but all was quiet on the Brantley front.

Matt texted me at 9:00 to say he was giving it 30 more minutes. I'd about had enough myself. I put my phone down and considered eating the granola bar that had been riding in my pack since the previous October. I decided against it, in favor of letting it age another year.

Then I looked up and saw him. A good buck was running flat out from the neighbor's farm, straight toward the box blind. I stopped him with a grunt and shot him through both lungs. He had 13 points, and his bases were as big around as Miller High Life cans. I realized that Michelle would soon see this deer, and that it wouldn't take her long to piece together that perhaps if she'd sat in that box blind as she'd requested, she would've killed the buck instead of me. Fortunately for me, Michelle is a seasoned hunter and saw the humor in the situation. "Congratulations, $#&%@!" she said as she flipped me the bird and walked back to camp, maybe to puke again.

A Euro mount of that 13-pointer hangs on the wall in the cabin. It was pure luck that he ran past me that morning, but shooting him came with some baggage. Matt jumps at every chance to tell anyone who'll listen: "That's the big buck Will stole from his pregnant wife." —W.B.

036 FRY UP THE BEST ELK EVER

Once, in a backcountry camp, I sliced up half an elk backstrap, rolled it in seasoned Bisquick, and fried it on the upturned lid of a Dutch oven. It was maybe the best thing I've ever eaten, not because of the Bisquick (I'd rather have used plain flour), but because we'd been hauling elk quarters out of the bottom of the next drainage over all morning. It was a 3-mile hike at 7,000 feet, and most of it in the rain.

My buddy and I stood outside the wall tent in our long underwear as our clothes dried over the wood stove. Light rain hit us in the face as we medicated aching muscles with cups of whiskey and tore into steaming, greasy elk steak with our bare hands. That moment, we agreed, was as good as life was likely to get. —W.B.

037 SPEAK CRITTER

My guide and I were crouched in a pit blind in eastern Arkansas, calling to a flock of circling mallards. One of the greenheads banked away from us and ejected a forceful squirt of white excrement that sprinkled down onto the flooded field. My guide dropped his call lanyard and reached for his coffee.

"He pooped. It's over."

In 20 years of calling ducks, I'd never heard such a thing. "If you're working mallards and they poop, it means they don't like something," he said. "Damn near guaranteed they've got your number and are leaving."

What's that have to do with calling elk, moose, or anything else? Everything. Being a good game caller means being able to replicate sounds, and the best ones do a good enough job of that, even if they might not be competition-level callers. What they're universally good at, though, is reading the animals and their cues, and letting the critters tell them what to do next.

Sometimes you need to call more urgently. Sometimes you'd best shut up and shoulder your gun. And sometimes—like when a duck poops or a bull bolts—it's time to drop the call, have a sip of coffee, and move on to the next opportunity. —W.B.

038 DON'T OVERTHINK IT

My first archery mule deer hunt out West wasn't unlike an early-season whitetail hunt back home in Kentucky. My buddy, Miles Fedinec, had found an alfalfa field full of deer (not to mention pronghorn and a few elk), and had been watching one particular 4-pointer for two weeks. The buck had a pretty frame and was, most important, predictable. We set up a ground blind at the edge of the alfalfa, near the trail he used most, and I killed him at 30 yards on the second evening of my hunt.

Miles still had a tag, and so we hunted hard the rest of that week in the more traditional western style. We spotted several bucks and made good stalks, but Miles never got a clear shot. "Sometimes, there's no need to overthink things," he said afterward. "Feed to bed, bed to feed. Figure that pattern out, and you can successfully hunt anything in the world."

Since then, I've seen ground-blind sets for elk, antelope shot from atop windmills, and moose that were patterned on open crop fields. None of that is what you might envision when planning a western big game hunt, but it all punched tags. The lesson, as always: Redneck ingenuity works everywhere. —W.B.

039 KNOW YOUR HORSE

The classic guided elk hunt typically involves horses and rugged public backcountry. Folks tend to envision all sorts of calamities on such hunts, from bear attacks to merciless mountain storms. But don't assume that old nag named Eeyore can't kill you just as easily. In fact, you're more likely to get hurt on the ride in or out of the mountains as you are out there in the great unknown. A lot of your riding will be done in the dark—and some of it across trails scantly wider than a horseshoe. One slip and you and your mount are goners.

I grew up around horses and still don't particularly like any of them. But they're a backcountry necessity. If you're planning a hunt out West and have never ridden before, a lesson at a local stable to learn the basics is money well spent.

Now that I've instilled more fear in you than a snake-handling preacher, here are a few general horsemanship rules to ensure your bull elk is the only carcass hauled from the woods.

STOP, DANG IT! In a perfect world, you'll be riding a properly broke horse. Stop the animal by getting a tight rein, firmly but quickly pulling back, and saying, "Whoa." Then let off the rein. If you keep pulling, the horse will often begin backing up or, worse, start to rear.

WEAR SPURS They are the great equalizer between you and the 1,000-pound farting beast underneath. You're not going to hurt the horse. A good poke with a spur simply reinforces who's in charge.

REAR UP? LEAN FORWARD A horse on two legs is the most dangerous kind. Never pull on the reins in this scenario. Instead, lean forward against the horse's neck to physically hinder it from falling back on top of you. Once all four hooves are back on the ground, dismount and ask for a different animal.

CENTER YOURSELF Go easy on your mount and it'll go easy on you. That means, in part, keeping a good center of gravity on inclines and declines. When you're going up a steep hill, lean forward in your saddle; lean back when heading downhill. —W.B.

040 LOSE THE GUT

If you live near sea level, as I do, you cannot realistically prepare your lungs for the rigors of hunting at high altitude, where oxygen is limited. But, if you're not in at least reasonable shape, your chances of killing a mountain critter aren't good.

For years, I've gone west each fall to hunt with my buddy and Colorado guide Miles Fedinec. He likes to make fun of the fact that where I live a pile of gravel constitutes a pretty good hill. He's 140 pounds of muscle, and while I can't keep up with him in the Rockies, I can at least keep him in sight, which is good enough for me.

To prepare for a hunt with Miles, I don't have to train like an Olympian. I run a couple miles a day, four or five days a week. I do some push-ups and sit-ups. I don't drink much soda or eat many sweets—though I do like beer and fried fish, and I'll be damned if I'm giving up either of them.

Cardio work—running, biking, swimming, and even walking—is the key to preparing for a mountain hunt. Doing some modest free-weight work from time to time

will help when it comes time to haul meat on your back. But the most important thing is not how far you run or how much you lift, but creating a routine. A mile-long jog every day for a year is better for your conditioning than a frantic 5-mile blitz and sprained ankle the month before your hunt. —W.B.

041 DECOY A PRONGHORN

If you've had more fun with a vinyl blow-up toy than I have, you need to talk to your preacher. Stalking pronghorns behind inflatable decoys was about the biggest hoot I've had hunting. Dominant bucks will charge from hundreds of yards away. Here's how two hunters get it done.

DO YOUR GLASS WORK Scout to find a stalkable goat. You'll need a good wind and terrain that will cover you to within a few hundred yards. One hunter grabs a bow, the other totes the doll baby.

GET IN POSITION Stay behind the decoy to keep from being busted by unseen animals. Use ridgelines, gullies, and vegetation to get close enough so that the first time the buck sees you is when the decoy-toting partner slips the deke over the ridge or into the open.

TAKE A KNEE While both hunters must stay behind the decoy, the archer should kneel for stability during the shot. Bucks often charge hard, then pull up short to parade back and forth. When a shot opportunity presents itself, the decoy handler slides the inflatable slightly out of the way as the bowman leans out, aims, and lets fly. —T.E.N.

HELL, I CAN SKIN THAT!

MOUNTAIN LION

A mountain lion represents both an incredible trophy and a fine meal. Here's one way to skin a cat.

CHECK IT Cat hunting is tightly regulated, and in many states a tagged lion must be visually inspected, aged, and documented by a wildlife agent. In some places they'll extract a tooth. Don't cut up anything without first knowing the regs.

GO UP AND OUT While field dressing and skinning, work your knife blade under the skin, and cut away from you with the knife's edge up (A). This mostly separates the hair instead of just slicing through it.

STAY INSIDE Cut along the rear edge of both of the cat's hind legs, down to the base of the tail (B). Cut off the paws at the joints, leaving them in the hide for your taxidermist (C). Cut along the inside of the front legs, down across the cat's chest, to meet the field-dress cut (D). Then finish skinning the animal. Most people cut off the cat's tailbone and head (E), leaving those delicate areas in the hide for the taxidermist. Leave proof of sex attached to the carcass as required by law.

QUARTER LIKE A DEER Once you've skinned away the stinky coat, the meat underneath is white and clean—similar to pork. The quarters, backstraps, and tenderloins are all there; remove them same as you would from a deer (F), and fry or grill.

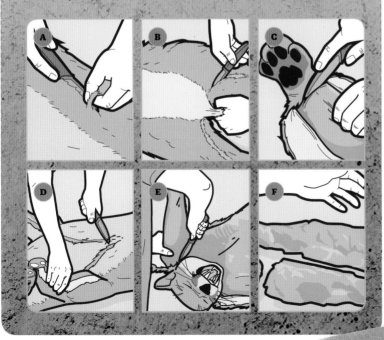

042 TAPE YOUR GATORS

One midnight a few years back, my wife, Michelle, and I were hunting alligators on a Florida river with our friends Tom and Ashley. I shot an 8-foot gator with a crossbow, and then hit him with the bang stick at boat side. We hauled him in, bleeding and seemingly dead, and continued scanning the shoreline with a spotlight, looking for orange eyes.

"Honey, that alligator is still alive," Michelle said half an hour later. Nah, Tom assured her. Alligators are apt to twitch a while. But Michelle argued with conviction. "This one's up walking."

We suddenly had a problem on our hands. Acting quickly, I got good purchase on the gator's tail while Tom jumped on the snout, which, of course, we hadn't taped. He held tight and flopped the front end of the gator overboard while I held on to the tail. The bang stick popped again in a splash of black water. The gator seemed dead enough, but then we'd already thought that once. To be safe, Tom wrapped his maw with several good pulls of duct tape. "From now on," said Tom, "no gator comes on board without a wrapped snout. That's one thing you don't get to relearn."—w.b.

043 BE A REDNECK GOURMET

If you can hunt it, chances are you can eat it. Here are our suggestions on when and how to serve up a few favorites, redneck-style.

THE MEAT	WHEN TO SERVE IT	A FAIL-SAFE FEAST
SQUIRREL	You're a college student weary from the constant gut purging brought on by cafeteria food.	Crock-Pot burgoo: When the pot gets low, top it up with canned veggies, broth, and another tree rat.
VENISON	It's potluck day at church, and you need ample food to minimize the gossip.	Pulled-venison roast: Season like Italian beef, slow-cook, and serve on a hoagie roll with cheese.
WILD TURKEY	You're trying to get a picky kid to eat without having to resort to threats.	Turkey nuggets: Deep-fry and serve them up with a side of ranch dressing.
UPLAND BIRDS	You want to cook something special for the missus.	Whole, plucked quail: Inject with creole butter and slow-roast.
WATERFOWL	One or more coolers of iced beer are present.	Grilled poppers: Strips of duck breast wrapped in bacon with jalapeño pepper, onion, and cream cheese.
WILD PIG	The family is in for a summertime reunion and you expect a good fist fight or two.	Pork shoulders: Season heavily with dry barbecue rub and smoke on low for 10-plus hours.

044 SNATCH A BEARD

You can carefully slice the beard off your trophy gobbler, but if you want to save time and impress your buddies, simply grab the beard at the base with one hand, press against the turkey's breast with the other, and give it a good, swift yank. The beard will pop loose with a small, fleshy base intact. Sprinkle a few salt granules on it, and it's ready to be displayed for years to come.

045 BLOW A WINGBONE YELPER

Back in the day, most turkey hunters blew a wingbone call because it was the cheapest call around. Made from a turkey's humerus, ulna, and radius bones, wingbone calls have a smooth sound that can fool toms that have gotten used to hearing the latest glass-and-carbon-fiber gadgets.

PUCKER UP Insert the small end of the call barely into your mouth, and press your lips firmly against the call's "mouth gauge"—a stop of hard plastic or wood.

CUP UP Hold the trumpet end between your thumb and a forefinger, and create a flared bell with the rest of the fingers. Cover with the cupped fingers and palm of the other hand. Vary hand positions to create different call tones.

SUCK UP To cluck, suck in air as if you're making a kissing sound. For yelps, suck in air with a very tight lip seal then drop the lower jaw to create the break of a hen yelp.

046 KILL THE FARM BIRD

I'm not talking the white turkey that's too fat to fly out of its pen. This is the tom that struts around in your farmer buddy's cow pasture every day. The one he insists he could shoot off the tractor with a .22 and can't understand why the heck you can't kill him.

The gobbler might be unafraid of the tractor, but he's one tough bird to call into shotgun range. He'll stare at your hen decoy and gobble at your every cluck without moving an inch your way. But you can still put one of his feathers in your cap. Here's how.

GET HIM DIALED Dedicate a day to just watching the bird and learning where he enters and exits the field. Could be he's pitching right into the open off the roost. Maybe he's not even showing up until mid morning. Regardless, even if it means waking up an hour earlier than normal or sitting half the day, you can probably kill this turkey by knowing where he'll be, settling in, and being patient.

CHALLENGE HIM A tom strutting with hens has no reason to come to your single fake hen—but a full-strut gobbler decoy can make his blood boil, especially if you're able to get within 100 yards before showing it to him. You can hide behind the decoy and stay where you are, or slowly creep toward him, "turkey reaper" style. When henned-up gobblers respond to a challenge like

this, it's often fast. (For safety reasons, never attempt this within gun range of a treeline, where another hunter could be waiting.)

PLAY THE FIGHT SONG A fighting purr can work when no other call will—but it can spook turkeys too, so use it as a last-ditch effort. The sound is a loud, rolling, aggressive purr made by two or more turkeys at once during a fight. I've heard live turkeys carry on for 10 minutes or more, but usually the fight and the sounds are over after a minute or so. A single caller can replicate the sound with a pair of push-pull-style box calls, like the classic Knight & Hale Fighting Ultimate Purr system. But it sounds better with two callers making noise on a pair of friction calls. Play this song for the right strutter and you'll have to end the fight with your 12-gauge.—W.B.

047 DRY A FAN

Though you could buy a fake fan, a dried fan from a real bird is best for dressing a full-strut gobbler decoy or for hiding your approach toward a strutting tom. And preparing a fan from a turkey you've killed couldn't be easier.

Simply find the joint of the tail at the base of the fan, part away the feathers below that joint (A), slice around it with your knife, and give it a gentle twist to pop it free.

Trim away excess, hanging flesh, but leave most of the fan base intact (B).

Splay the fan out on a piece of cardboard and secure it in place with staples or pins (C). Saturate the fleshy base with salt or borax, let it sit for two weeks in a dry place, and—boom—you're ready to fool your next gobbler.

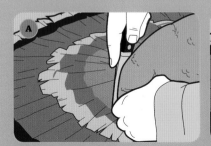

048 MAKE A MOCK DUSTING BOWL

Wild turkeys will roll in loose, dry soil like a dog in a coon carcass. Some say that it's to help rid themselves of parasites, while others figure they're working the dirt into oily feathers and then shaking it out to help clean their plumage. Either way, opening a gobbler day spa near a favorite hunting location is a dirty trick that works.

CHOOSE YOUR SPOT First, locate turkey sign near a bare piece of ground with a southern exposure that will help keep the soil dry. Great options include clear-cuts, utility line rights-of-way, and field edges where birds travel between feeding and roosting areas.

BUILD YOUR BATH Use a garden trowel to break up the ground in a 4-foot-long oval. Crumble the dirt clods to powder.

STAKE IT OUT After a morning hunt, post up near the dust bowl and call occasionally. You might draw in a peeping tom wanting to eyeball a few dirt-bathing beauties.

049 BLITZ A MOUNTAIN BIRD

Some of the country's toughest turkeys live in the mountains. Eric Brock has spent a lifetime hunting the ones that reside in the Appalachians.

"Normally we park at the bottom of the mountain so we have more options for getting to a bird, depending on where he gobbles," says Brock. "Plus, it's nice to have a downhill walk back to the truck. But you always have a steep climb ahead of you first thing in the morning."

It doesn't matter if a gobbling bird is sitting atop the next ridge over—Brock is going to him. Being in top physical shape is an absolute requirement. "Lots of things can go wrong and keep you from killing a turkey. You never want physical limitations to be one of them."

Henned-up toms frequently roost at lower elevations, but Brock says lone toms often roost higher and gobble more often. The trick to killing one is to get on his level or above him. The faster you can do that without spooking the bird, the better your odds.

"A good setup is the key to killing a mountain turkey. We set up behind breaks in the terrain so that when he appears, he's in gun range. But you can't sit too close to a break, or he'll slip in on you and spook at 5 yards before you can ever get a shot," says Brock.

"Ideally, you'll sit on the edge of a little flat or logging road and call him out onto that. But you have to take what you're given. There have been times when I've had to dig my heels in to keep from sliding down the side of a mountain while I was working a turkey," he says.

050 PICK A HEN FIGHT

A clear morning broke on the final day of the season without us hearing a single gobble. My wife and I were sitting over a food plot with a hen decoy staked in front of us. I made a few loud yelps, and a live hen on the limb answered from 60 yards behind us. For the next 15 minutes, she interrupted my every yelp with evermore aggressive yelping of her own. Finally, she pitched into the plot and began circling the decoy. "Longbeard coming!" Michelle whispered.

Sure enough, a tom was coming right to us—from across the road. He walked to within 20 yards without ever making a sound. Unfortunately, he caught Michelle slightly out of position and she missed. Still, it reinforced one of the few rules of turkey calling that I follow 100 percent of the time: When a hen answers me, I mock her immediately. The more she calls, the louder and more obnoxiously I answer. Eventually, she'll come in for a fight. There is no deadlier sound in the spring woods than two hens screaming at one another. I've literally seen it pull a gobbler across a blacktop road. —W.B.

051 DOUBLE LIKE A PRO

One of my best career moves ever was calling up a pair of 2-year-old gobblers for the editor-in-chief of *Field & Stream*. Randy young toms can make any chump with a box call look like a hero—and since they often travel in packs, they provide golden opportunities for doubles. Here's how to do it.

SET UP FOR SATELLITES Groups of subordinate toms are roamers. They'll check every food plot, hardwood ridge, and hayfield on their home turf for hens, and they'll do plenty of gobbling along the way. Hit likely fields and ridges, call aggressively, and wait for that string of eager, overlapping gobbles. Set up about 5 yards from your partner, so that each of you has enough room to safely swing a gun but so you're still able to communicate. To grab the attention of the bird, stake a hen decoy 25 yards out, and position it perfectly for your shots.

PLAN THE SHOTS Don't be shy on the call. Pull these gobblers into the open where they can see your decoy, and odds are they'll strut right into range. Once they do, don't bother with the old "One, two, three, SHOOT!" maneuver. That rarely works. Instead, let your partner shoot first and hope he has the decency to kill the turkey on his side. Even if you don't have an immediate shot, you should be able to knock down a second bird with relative ease. Typically, the surviving turkeys will scatter at the shot and then stand around for a few seconds within gun range for a bit. Several times, I've seen the stragglers rush in to flog the dead tom. Both are easy opportunities for a crack shot like you. And even if you don't go home with a bird, you still might get a raise.—W.B.

052 COOK GOBBLER HOT WINGS

For an easy, can't-miss recipe that can be enjoyed sober but is best paired with cheap beer, consider making wild turkey "wings" out of boneless breast meat. First, slice and trim the meat into finger-size strips, then wash and pat dry. Roll the strips in seasoned flour, then lightly pan-fry them in olive oil. Meanwhile, prepare your dipping sauce. I prefer Frank's Redhot mixed with melted butter, but my wife and boy like barbecue sauce and melted honey. Make a little of both.

When the nuggets are lightly browned, remove them from the skillet and liberally coat them with the sauce. Spread them out on a cookie sheet lined with parchment paper, and bake them for 30 minutes at 325°F. Serve with ranch or blue cheese dressing on the side.—W.B.

053 SWITCH IT UP WITH AN OLD-SCHOOL CALL

Your granddaddy didn't need a jaw full of latex to kill a turkey, and his old go-to calls will still get pressured and close-mouthed toms talking. Try one of these the next time a battle-scarred gobbler ignores your mouth rubber.

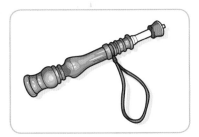

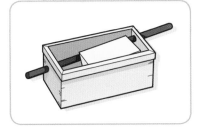

TRUMPET Similar to wingbone yelpers in design and function, trumpets are made of exotic woods, metal, or glass and plastic. They're known for full, natural sounds with a louder edge than those made by wingbones, which do a good job of slicing through windy mornings.

PUSH-BUTTON These require little skill. You simply push on a striker rod that causes a small paddle to rub against an internal structure. They're fickle in the rain, but they produce fine clucks, purrs, and yelps. Some can be mounted to a shotgun and used when the gun is shouldered to entice hung-up gobblers to take those last crucial steps.

TUBE CALL This call comprises a piece of latex stretched over the opening of a container such as a film canister or snuff box, and held in place with the container's lid or a rubber band. In the right hands, every wild turkey sound can be made with a tube call, from gobbles to kee kee runs.

054 FRY A BIRD WHOLE

Place your frying rig safely away from structures, on a nonflammable surface, like dirt or concrete. Check how much oil you'll need by putting the turkey in your frying rig, adding water to about a half inch over the bird. Mark the line, then pour out the water and dry the pot and bird thoroughly. Fill the pot with peanut oil to the line you marked and heat to about 350°F. Season the bird liberally and insert the hanger into it. Once the oil is hot enough, lower the bird in slowly and carefully. Fry for about three minutes per pound of bird, until the internal temperature reaches 145°F. Then pull it out and let it rest about 20 minutes before carving. Your fried turkey will get all the table glory it deserves, and you can invite the whole family over to feast on the bird and get belligerently drunk—just like at Thanksgiving.

055 KNOW YOUR TARGET

Rednecks enjoy solving problems with firearms. Though you can't shoot your way out of an invasive feral hog infestation, you can have fun trying. Nighttime thermal-vision hog hunts are all the rage right now, and they may be the best time you can have in a Deep South peanut field after dark. But, given you're firing a high-powered rifle in the dark at living targets you can't see without the aid of technology, hiring a competent guide is all but mandatory. At least for your first time out.

I once shot pigs for a couple nights in Georgia with the guys from Jager Pro, as good of a group of wild swine eradicators as you'll find. After gunning down a trailer load of hogs, here's what I learned.

SPRING FORTH Early spring is a great time to hunt, since this is when large crop fields are planted and pigs are most visible. Once the foliage gets thick, shooting becomes more difficult.

USE ENOUGH GUN ARs dominate this game, but your .223 isn't enough "pumpkin" to knock down big hogs on the run. The Jager Pro guys shoot AR-10s in .308, and so does about everyone else who knows what they're doing.

LISTEN UP Most thermal-vision optics are activated by applying pressure to the eyepiece, so using them is contrary to how you've learned to sight through a scope. Furthermore, the view through your scope will be a heat signature. Hogs should look like hogs, but deer, dogs, coyotes, and other critters can look a bit like hogs too. Familiarize yourself with your gun and optic on the range in the daylight. After dark, when your guides tell you to do something, listen to them. —w.b.

056 SHOOT A ROTISSERIE PIGLET

Bite into the stringy chop of a rank wild boar, and you'll learn why serious pig hunters like to shoot the little ones. Wild pigs grow fast. A two-month-old shoat will weigh around 30 pounds—just big enough to gain a little fat, and young enough for fork-tender barbecue. Such a pig, shot in the head, can be roasted whole on the spit or split down the middle to fit on the racks of your smoker.

057 STICK A WILD PIG

Long before Hogzilla was hauled out of Georgia's swamps, Hawaiian natives were knifing wild Polynesian pigs. Maui native Rodney Perreira Jr. guides hunters in close combat, where they put a Bowie into bayed bacon.

SNEAKY SNEAK Approach the pig from the rear while it's focused on the dogs. Move slowly and avoid getting between your quarry and anything that would prevent you from backing away from the fight.

HERE, HOLD THIS Grab the pig's hind legs just above the hoof. Lift the animal up like a wheelbarrow. "Now you have control," Perreira says. Flip him over on his side. It's easier than you think. "The pig's strength is in his back legs," Perreira explains, "and you've taken that away."

COUP DE GRÂCE Let go with your knife hand and get a knee on the pig's shoulder, just behind where you'd place a bullet on a deer. Sink the knife low and behind the shoulder.

058 READ SWINE SIGN

Have hogs infiltrated your deer lease's hardwood bottom? Here are four things to look for.

TRACKS A hog track is more rounded or blunt than a deer's pointed track. Look for slightly triangular prints.

WALLOWS Hogs love to wallow, so give muddy slicks the sniff test: Hogs urinate and defecate in their wallows, so it's easy to tell if you've found a pig spa.

RUBS Hogs rub against trees, fence rails, logs, and rocks to scratch irritated skin or remove parasites and dried mud. The freshness of mud left behind indicates how long since the pig passed by.

ROOTING A sounder can churn acres overnight. The only thing that comes close is a flock of turkeys. Upturned leaves in roughly circular patches mean turkey. Rooting hogs rip the ground to shreds.

059 PULL OFF A BEAR DRIVE

Penn State's Tau Phi Delta fraternity has a meat pole, game freezers, and an archery range in the side yard, and the house turns into a hunt camp for Pennsylvania's Thanksgiving-week bear season. They hunt bruins the traditional way, too, with pushers and standers getting it done in the gnarly Penn woods.

I was there one November when two dozen brothers and alumni pulled off the highway at dawn. The veterans wore shin guards and knee braces. "I did this last year," said one, shaking his head at the rough forested country ahead. "I can't believe anything lives on that f-#*%$@ mountain."

Here's how they put bears on the ground.

WORK AS A TEAM Hunters draw numbers for push and stand positions. "Nobody says, 'I've got to kill a bear,'" one brother explained. "It's all about the we."

ASSUME POSITIONS Everyone climbs in total silence. Standers drop off first, forming a straight line down the steep flank. Pushers continue on a half mile, then do the same. At a predetermined time, they close the vise.

HOLD THE LINE If a pusher bogs down, the directive rings out: "Hold the line!" The line must remain straight no matter what.

BE SMART Standers watch even the smallest opening. One bear was killed when a stander lay on the ground to look below the brush, saw four black paws, stood up, and killed the bear at 12 yards.

KEEP MOVING After the first push, leave a small group to deal with any downed bear, then move quickly to reassemble a second drive to catch bears dislodged from nearby thickets. —T.E.N.

060 BAIT A BEAR WITH BACON

A good black bear bait might include marshmallows, used cooking oil, doughnuts, even a festering beaver carcass hung from a tree, but the greatest ones use bacon. Bear baits need to be kept active to remain productive, and many guides will fry bacon upwind from a bait site whenever they go freshen a set. They simply pack in a single-burner stove (like a Jetboil) and a small skillet, and sear the pork before moving in to freshen the bait.

That smell of frying bacon makes bears go weak in the knees—same as you and me—and they will quickly learn to associate it with a smorgasbord of fresh chow. Once on the bacon plan, it doesn't hurt to fry up a skillet full of pig upwind of your stand just before you settle in to hunt. Just don't be at all surprised if your bear shows up within minutes.

061 KILL A BEAR WITH AN $8 KNIFE

Pray that you never have to be as tough as Minnesota strongman Brandon Johnson. Around midnight on September 27, 2014, Johnson was helping a friend blood-trail a 525-pound black bear. Johnson doesn't remember the wounded bruin's initial charge, but he remembers the rest.

"When I snapped out of the shock, I had my hands around the bear's muzzle as it knocked me down in the mud and latched onto my face. I had a knife in my right hand and I stabbed it in the bear's face, and stabbed and stabbed as hard and as fast as I could. All of a sudden, it was gone.

"On the second charge he came straight for my crotch, biting and clawing. I locked my knees, so he charged up to my chest again. He slammed my left arm away and opened his mouth so wide his pupils rolled up into his head. I remember his teeth and these white spots where his eyes were supposed to be, and I thought: *This is it.* I heard what I thought was my buddy stepping on a stick. It turned out to be my left arm snapping.

"I kept stabbing and stabbing with this $8 flea-market knife. He had my broken arm in his mouth when he spun around, twisting my wrist all the way around inside the skin, and he snapped my thumb and tore all the ligaments.

"The bear backed away, and all the hope was draining out of my body like water in a tub. When he ran back in I had just enough time to use my good right hand to drape my broken left arm over my face, and with all the strength I had left I shoved the knife so far down his throat that I broke two fingers.

"I kept stabbing. I was choking on blood. He chomped down twice on my right arm, and broke it. All I could do then was wave the knife back and forth in front of him, and he swatted my broken arms apart, smacked me in the chest, grabbed my right calf, and slammed me into the ground.

"Then he left for good. Searchers found him bled out about 45 yards away. His head was resting on his crossed paws as if he'd been lying there watching me die."

062
KNOW WHERE THE BIG BEARS LIVE

In 1998, Dolly Parton's cousin Coy Parton trucked his bear dogs from Tennessee to eastern North Carolina and shot an 880-pound black bear, which still stands as the heaviest known black bear ever taken in North America. In fact, the planet's biggest black bears don't live in Canada or Alaska but close enough to the beach to smell the Banana Boat in the air.

Hunters have taken more than a dozen 700-pound black bears in the North Carolina coastal plain, supersize bruins that gorge themselves fat and happy on a virtual Golden Corral buffet for omnivores. Carolina bays and huge swamps, called pocosins, are thick with huckleberries, gallberries, blackberries, and blueberries. The swamps are surrounded by vast fields of wheat, corn, and soybeans. Commercial hog farms dispose of carcasses in giant waste bins—it's like a Chocolate Waterfall to a binge-eating bear. If you want a rug the size of a circus tent, you're wise to head south, not north.

GETTING THE MOOSE HOME

Devin wanted to drive his Jeep across the beaver pond, but I talked him out of it. It had been an exceptionally rainy autumn in northern Alberta, and though the Canuck's confidence was inspiring, we were staring across a brown-water abyss. "It's 2 miles up that trail on the other side to the good hunting," he said. It was 30 miles in the other direction to the nearest help—his mother's house.

"I'm good with walking, buddy," I said.

He stuck a bottle of water and a gas station lighter—his survival gear for the day—in his pocket. "Well, let's go then."

We found fresh moose tracks and rubs almost immediately, and we were onto a good bull a half hour later. I dropped him when he crossed a logging road 180 yards away. I'd assumed we'd quarter and carry him out to the Jeep a piece at a time, but Devin had a better idea: He would summon his mother to help.

"She's got an Argo and a quad, and a chainsaw, too," he said. "We'll drive it all right across the beaver pond and get him out of here like that. To hell with carrying meat. Probably take me about four hours to get the machines in here, though."

"I'll have this big sucker cut up before you get back," I said.

I broke two knife blades and strained an ass muscle removing the first quarter, which weighed as much as a whitetail doe. But I rendered one side of the bull and cut off the head. It took a log wedged under the moose's rear end and substantial swearing to roll it over and work on the other side. I was on the final quarter when I heard machines in the distance. Devin and his mother were an hour ahead of schedule.

She was a petite and lovely lady, and she had a chainsaw strapped to the front rack of her quad. Devin followed behind her in the Argo. She immediately walked up and lifted the moose's front leg to help me slice off the shoulder. "Don't miss that neck meat," she said. "It's a good roast."

We piled the meat and skull into the Argo's tiny rear cargo area. Devin insisted on taking the torso full of guts, too, for wolf bait. He ran a chain through the rib cage and hooked it to the back of the machine, which stalled out within 50 yards.

"Honey, I think you'll have to leave those guts here," his mother said. Devin looked hurt at the suggestion, but he undid the chain and vowed to return the next day. It was, after all, several hundred pounds of good guts.

I thought he'd check up at the beaver pond, but he hit it full-throttle. The quarter ton of meat nearly swamped us. With maybe an inch of freeboard in the rear, I sprawled myself across the hood of the Argo to keep the machine afloat while Devin slogged through waist-deep water to secure the winch cable to a spruce. "Just take her easy," he said. There was no other way to take her. I'd never driven an Argo, but gradually, with the help of the winch, I steered it out of the muck.

Devin's mother, balanced on her knees on the quad's gas tank, plowed into the icy pond. I'm not sure the front wheels ever touched bottom. Devin was screaming, "Give it hell, Ma!" and hell is precisely what Ma gave. Acrid steam boiled off the engine when she came to a stop on our bank. But she was perfectly dry.

"Honey, you're soaked," she said to Devin. He lit a cigarette, and I could tell it was a struggle for her not to get after him. She was, after all, his mother.

"I'm fine," he said. "But we better get this meat on back."

Sunset was only an hour away by the time we reached her house. "I'm glad you got your moose," she said to me. I wanted to pay her for her time, but she'd only accept a roast and a hug. That's the way it usually is with rednecks. Eager to help, and fully capable of doing so.—W.B.

UPLAND BIRDS

We call them upland birds because they don't live on the water. The group includes quail, grouse, and pheasants, but we'll toss in doves as well. It'd be hard to invent a better class of creatures for the everyday redneck to hunt. You can corner most of them with a pointing dog, and shoot them on the rise. Or you can kick them out of the bushes with brush pants and sweat, and knock them down with your granddaddy's Iver Johnson. These are farm-field birds and ditch-bank birds and back-40 woods birds. You don't have to put on airs to put on a chase, and you don't have to have a lot of money to get after them.

A lot of folks cut their hunting teeth on upland birds, and a lot forget about them once they get bit by the bigger-game bug. We call that a shame, because these birds won't cost you a thing but a box of shells and a couple hours of walking. —T.E.N.

063 HUNT DITCH PARROTS WITHOUT A DOG

The most memorable pheasant I ever killed flushed out of the picked-clean bones of a cow carcass. I was pushing a tangle of weeds and abandoned farm trucks behind a run-down tractor shed in the Texas Panhandle. There wasn't a dog within a half mile, proving you don't have to have a pointer or flusher to shoot roosters. But you need a plan.

GREET THE SUN Hunt early while birds are feeding in relatively thin cover, and before bird dogs and other hunters drive them into the thick stuff. Zero in on cover near dirt roads. Pheasants often head to gravel first thing in the morning to pick up grit, and you can kick them out of ditch banks.

WALK THE LINE Move quickly when working long, narrow lines of cover, such as shelterbelts and fence thickets. Don't stomp around and pout each time a bird flushes out the other side. Get to the end, where pheasants will hole up thinking the coast is clear.

THROTTLE BACK When walking more open field cover, slow down, zigzag, and pause plenty. Doing so can send a nervous, hunkered-down rooster into flight. Stop before you get to the end of a field and stand quietly for a couple minutes. Fidgety birds can't take the pressure and will fly before your final push.

ZERO IN Brush piles and scrubby islands surrounded by fields suck in the birds. Work them like you'd kick bunnies out of a briar patch. Comb the outer edges first for nervous Nellies that will flush at the first snapping twig, then suck it up and wade into the thick stuff.

AMBUSH THE ROOST Birds will move to roosting cover during the last hour of daylight. Work the edges of Conservation Reserve Program (CRP) fields as the sun drops.

BE THE DOG The only thing tougher than putting a pheasant into the air without a dog is retrieving any downed birds on your own. Take the high-percentage shots only, and never shoot more than one bird at a time. Mark where the bird goes down, and get there as quickly as you can. Look and listen for rustling in the cover, and bird-dog the pheasant till it's in your hand. —T.E.N.

064 MASTER THE GROUND SWAT

Watching his high-dollar bird dog work an alder thicket, my Maine guide couldn't help but laugh. "I didn't know grouse could fly till I was 25 years old," said Tim Winslow. "Everybody shot 'em on the ground, and nobody thought a thing about it."

The ground swat is a hallowed tradition in many grousey corners of Redneck America. Some folks figure shooting a bird on the ground ranks down there with kicking kittens, but a lot of good people think it's as natural as peeing off the back porch. I'd never shoot a bird from the truck, and I'd far rather shoot grouse on the wing. But after six hours of being a good boy that day in Maine, I got fed up with one pa'tridge in particular.

He ran through 80 yards of spruce hell without the good manners to flap a wing. I shot that sucker when he was about to squirm through another morass of dark timber, and I didn't feel one bit dirty. It's legal in most places, so if you're up for the occasional ground sluice or limb level, make it clean. Check for dogs, other hunters, buildings, and endangered woodpeckers in harm's way, then get you some groceries. —T.E.N.

065 TEACH A DOG TO TRAIL

Used to be, every other house on a dirt road had a hound dog that could smell its way to a treed coon or a crippled bird. It's not a common skill these days, but you can train a sniffing machine yourself.

MAKE A DRAGGING POLE Run 10 feet of parachute cord through a 5-foot length of PVC pipe, and attach one end of the cord to a training dummy. Use the pipe to hold the dummy away from your body as you lay down the scent trail.

STINK IT UP Start downwind with 10-yard, straight-line retrieves on short grass. Gradually increase the difficulty with curved drag lines, taller grasses, abrupt turns, and short gaps in the scent trail.

TREAT SUCCESS If you need to use treats to keep your dog excited, use them sparingly. After all, the point is to find the big payoff at the end of the trail, not the Vienna sausages along the way.

GO TO GRAD SCHOOL Dial up the challenge. Run the scent trail along a log as if the wounded bird ran down it. Drag it in and out of a creek or pond edge. Create longer gaps.

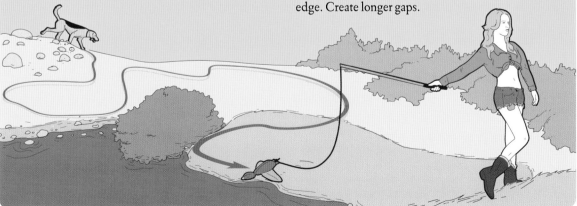

066 PREPARE A DOVE FEAST

All proper dove shoots are followed by a big lunch; and, when available, grilled dove breasts are a menu staple. Marinate the doves (bone-in for more flavor; boneless for less hassle) with Allegro marinade, then season to taste with salt, pepper, garlic powder, and Cajun seasoning. Stack on jalapeño slices and small chunks of cheddar cheese, wrap with half strips of thick bacon, and secure each with a toothpick. Top the toothpick ends with onion slices and grill to medium-rare perfection.

Don't know from Allegro marinade? You're missing out on a classic that's been "making inexpensive meat dinners more edible" since 1955 (and we're quoting from their website here). Much more edible, by which we mean delicious. Find it in your local store, or chase it down on the Internet.

067 AMBUSH BIRDS AT PONDS AND PINES

Didn't get invited back to the annual dove slam this year? Could have been those ATV doughnuts you carved into the field last year during one of your better butt-showing moves. Here's a dove-smacking backup plan that's so good it might just become your Opening Day Plan A: Doves have to drink every day, and they frequently pick up grit along roadsides and bare field and pond edges. Scout ponds with some bare ground and shade-giving pines nearby, and you can shoot a dove limit without breaking a sweat.

068 SHOOT FOR THE BEST DAY

September 1 is the traditional dove opener in most states, and it's no doubt the most popular day to hold a dove shoot. That doesn't mean it's always the best day to kill doves, however. Doves are migratory, and it doesn't take much of an early cold front to move big numbers of birds in—or out—of a field.

Like any hunting worth doing, scouting is important. If your field is loaded with birds on August 28 and the forecast is stable, plan the shoot. If a cold front will be blasting through, however, you might be better off to wait and let the migrant birds behind the front establish themselves in your field. When possible, time your shoot for the same day as others in the area. If there's a field 2 miles down the road with no hunters, the area birds will probably just pile into it and stay put once you start shooting. But gunfire in both fields should keep birds in the air most of the day.

069 PUT BIRDS ON A WIRE

Rednecks are a peaceful, rule-following people and would never use a live power or telephone wire as a dove decoy perch. But abandoned, out-of-service lines? That's a different story. Put two dove decoys on a wire, and you can melt a shotgun barrel. This technique also works to hoist decoys into bare tree branches.

I keep a small bag in my truck stuffed with everything I need to raise a few birds: a full spool of cheap 8-pound monofilament fishing line, a handful of 2- and 4-ounce pyramid fishing weights, some cheap aluminum tent stakes, and two dove decoys. Here's how to set it up.

STEP 1 Tie a weight to the end of the fishing line. I use a large spool so I can hold one side as I hurl the weight, and the line spools off the other side without snagging. Be careful as the weight drops to the ground that it doesn't swing and bash your noggin.

STEP 2 Remove the weight and tie a decoy to the line. Hoist it up snug to the wire.

STEP 3 Cut the line from the spool and tie it to a tent stake sunk into the ground.

STEP 4 Repeat the entire process with your other decoy. —T.E.N.

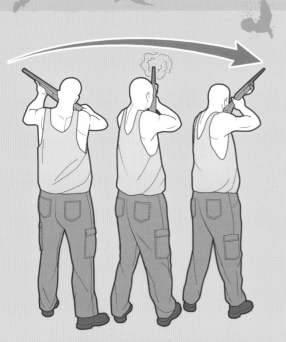

070 BE A SWINGER

It's hard to concentrate during an opening-day dove shoot, what with all the noobs sniping low-flying birds, that jackass Jimbo rolling up in his new Hemi, and half a dozen college kids in Daisy Dukes and knee boots running around. But the basics still apply. You gotta move that barrel, swing and keep swinging, and never take your focus off the bird.

There are tons of tricks to help you move your muzzle. For shooters using the swing-through method, mentally reciting "butt-belly-beak-bang" as you swing through the target will help carry the muzzle forward after the shot. For pull-away shooting at long-distance birds, I literally spell the word "dove" as I accelerate the bead away from the bird, like I'm writing D-O-V-E in the air. —T.E.N.

071 KNOW WHAT YOUR BIRD DOG SAYS ABOUT YOU

You've heard the phrase "that dog won't hunt." Heck, you've probably said it yourself. But what does your dog say about you? Here's the message you might be sending with ol' Rover.

YOUR DOG IS A . . .	RIGHT NOW YOU'RE . . .	YOU DRIVE A . . .
POINTER	Making fun of sissy field trial dogs.	Mid-90s Tacoma with mud tires. You'd like a new truck, but you're still making payments on the dog. Plus, this one never gets stuck.
SETTER	Drowning pancakes with maple syrup —the real stuff, which you tapped from a tree yourself. Hunting Yankee grouse calls for an epic breakfast.	GMC Sierra with a camper shell. Your wife gives you hell for your "old man truck," but it keeps the dogs warm and the gear dry. Plus, you're actually getting old.
LABRADOR RETRIEVER	Wrapping mallard breasts in bacon and showing your buddies how well you've trained Bowser to fetch beers from the fridge.	Dodge Ram with a $400 cooler in the bed and a DU decal on the back glass. The cooler is riddled with chew marks. It might be grizzly bear–proof, but it ain't Lab puppy–proof.
CHESAPEAKE BAY RETRIEVER	Insisting to the mailman that the dog "Hardly ever bites anyone that hard."	Big damn boat.
BRITTANY SPANIEL	Secretly wishing your dog had a longer tail, because watching that nub when a pheasant is close gives you motion sickness.	Full-size car that reeks of wet bird dog on the inside. Your kids have an entire bench-style back seat to themselves. The Brittany rides up front.
STANDARD POODLE	Writing in a small notebook all the reasons why Curls really is a bird dog.	Land Rover. Look, man, you're doing all this to yourself.

WATERFOWL

Every duck hunt has the same traits in common, no matter who's shooting. A couple winters ago, I ended a duck season by hunting with Bo Whoop, the legendary shotgun once owned by outdoor writer Nash Buckingham, now valued at more than $200,000. I shared the blind with rich businessmen, all of whom could shoot a shotgun, blow a duck call, and cuss admirably.

A year later, I stood in flooded timber next to a 22-year-old bearded Arkansan, his cheeks smudged in black paint. He could also blow a call, cuss, and shoot—but he carried a cheap pump gun and depended on his daily guide rate to support his 3-week-old son.

Waterfowling can seem genteel, but that's only a veneer. Field-trial champions and meat dogs alike inevitably take their predawn dumps upwind of the blind. No matter what, duck hunting is still a game of mud and boats, dogs and shotguns—things that all rednecks can appreciate. —W.B.

072 CLEAN A DUCK CALL

A duck call is made of only a few key parts: the barrel, the tone board, the reed(s), and the wedge (the last three parts collectively form the end piece). Eventually, the call will become clogged with chewing tobacco and breakfast burrito, so you'll need to know how to clean it. Here's how.

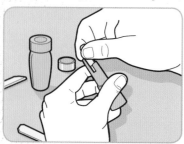  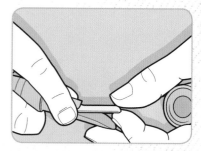

TAKE IT INSIDE It's best to clean your call on a clean table indoors, where you can spread the pieces before you. Start by removing the end piece from the barrel. If the call has a floating wedge, be sure to use a permanent marker to make a reference mark of where the reeds rest against the wedge before you pull the call completely apart.

WASH IT COLD Clean the call with plain cold water. Most duck call reeds are made of Mylar, which can be damaged by hot water and soap. Use a wet towel to clean wooden barrels (avoid soaking them), but plastic or acrylic barrels can be washed under a faucet. Let everything dry at room temperature before reassembling.

TUNE IT UP If your call has a J-frame-style backstop, reassembly is easy; simply put it back together in reverse order. If your call has a floating wedge, use your reference mark to position the reeds and wedge against the tone board, then press the end piece into the barrel. Next, make sure everything sounds correct. Moving the reeds forward or back can change the tone and pitch.

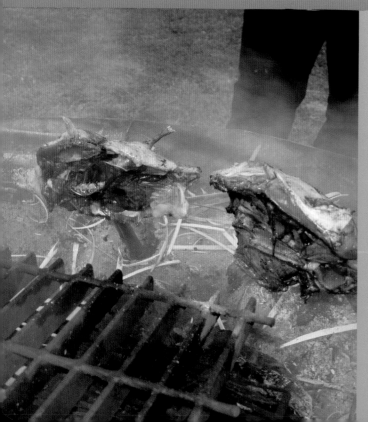

073 COOK DUCK ON A STICK

The best hunt-camp duck I ever ate was skewered on a stick and jammed into the smoldering fire of a Chipewyan boreal forest compound. Surrounded by half-burned cigarette cartons and a charred piece of truck chassis, the bird self-basted in its own dripping fat, which scorched in the fire and sent seasoning plumes of smoke around the meat. Yumbelievable.

Butterfly a plucked duck through the breast, not the back. Insert a stout knife along one side of the breastbone keel, cutting all the way to the backbone. Loosen up the bones by working the duck back and forth between your hands, as if you're trying to break a green stick. Flatten it with the palm of your hand. Skewer the duck by running a stick through the breast meat on one side of the keel, then the other. Anchor the stick in the ground at a 45-degree angle over the fire. Cook breast side to the fire first, then the back. —T.E.N.

074 KNOW THE RULES OF PUBLIC LAND

Public-land duck hunters are seriously confrontational. For better or worse, it's part of the experience; thankfully, confrontations rarely escalate past words. However, a hunting buddy of mine used to keep a fighting ring—a polished heavy-equipment lug nut—in his pocket. He'd engraved his initials into the ring so that "any son of a bitch I hit in the dark will know it was me come sunrise."

To avoid unpleasantness, simply follow these rules.

GET THERE FIRST, HUNT THERE FIRST Who gets to hunt where is the source of 95 percent of public-land duck hunting disputes. If someone beats you to a spot, find somewhere else to hunt.

DON'T MESS WITH OTHERS' SWINGS It's not hard to tell when birds are working someone else. Firing or calling at high birds swinging around on another man's spread will eventually earn you a special sort of lesson.

DON'T BE LATE The first 30 minutes of shooting light are sacred. Don't fumble around in your boat at that time.

DON'T BLOCK THE RAMP Keep your boat off the ramp until your gear is loaded and you're ready to motor away. And this is no time to teach your kid how to back a trailer.

CONTROL YOUR DOG Your retriever's bloodline may be impeccable, but your competition probably doesn't want him siring a litter with their gyp as they're preparing to head to the blind. Fundamental obedience training is best learned at home.

DON'T SKYBUST Regardless of what choke and premium load you've got, shooting farther than 40 yards usually results in wounded or educated birds—two things no real hunter cares for.

KEEP IT TO YOURSELF Yes, it's technically public land. But if a buddy shows you his secret spot, and you show up there the next day with a bunch of your other buddies, that's a great way to end up with his initials below your eye. —W.B.

075 SHOOT BEAVER- SWAMP DUCKS

God had us redneck duck hunters in mind when he made beaver swamps. Muck, mud, and catbrier. Downed logs as slick as otter snot. You won't catch sissy waterfowlers humping gear through a hellish beaver slough. The good news is that they're everywhere, from sedge-rimmed Minnesota ponds to Georgia swamps home to mosquitoes the size of greenwing teal. And you don't have to have a boat, a dog, or a pickup truck full of decoys to give it a shot. Just pack a machete and a pair of Kevlar underwear. And a fast-pointing gun, because this is quick-draw, in-your-face duck shooting. When it all comes together, it comes together big.

FIND YOUR SPOT Gunning a beaver pond starts with finding the right one. Young ponds and flooded swamps are a hunter's best bet, because rich, flooded soils produce a flush of edible plants. If your favorite pond seems to be drawing fewer ducks, then look up and down the watershed for any places where beavers have recently migrated.

However, even older ponds can offer a fine duck shoot. The surrounding trees produce more mast as they grow, providing a wood duck bonanza. As a beaver pond ages, it also tends to expand as the beavers add to the dam. Those deeper waters stay ice-free longer, and they can be a late-winter magnet when surrounding ponds freeze up.

Always scout beaver swamps in the morning, not the evening. An older beaver pond or swamp that fills with ducks roosting at sunset might be empty of birds just a few minutes past legal shooting light as they depart for distant feeding grounds.

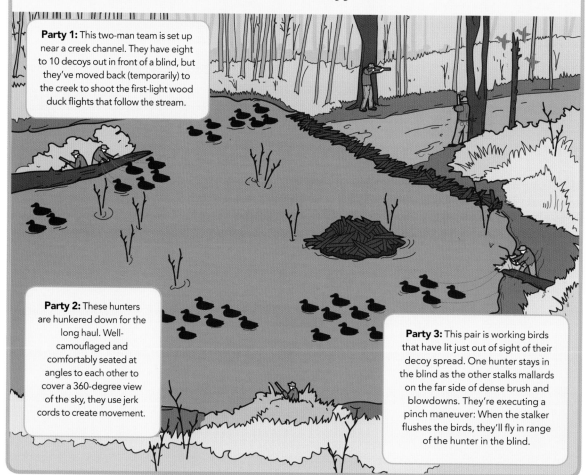

Party 1: This two-man team is set up near a creek channel. They have eight to 10 decoys out in front of a blind, but they've moved back (temporarily) to the creek to shoot the first-light wood duck flights that follow the stream.

Party 2: These hunters are hunkered down for the long haul. Well-camouflaged and comfortably seated at angles to each other to cover a 360-degree view of the sky, they use jerk cords to create movement.

Party 3: This pair is working birds that have lit just out of sight of their decoy spread. One hunter stays in the blind as the other stalks mallards on the far side of dense brush and blowdowns. They're executing a pinch maneuver: When the stalker flushes the birds, they'll fly in range of the hunter in the blind.

PREP BEFORE DAYLIGHT This is close-quarters combat, so concealment is critical. Gloves and face camo are absolutes. Tuck into brush, and use pruning shears and a small saw to trim away overhanging brush or briars that could snag your coat sleeve. If possible, try to face a horizon with views of open sky. A lot of birds sneak in below the dark treeline, even after first shooting light.

TAKE THE MAGIC HOUR Beaver pond birds can arrive very early, especially wood ducks. Set your phone alarm (on vibrate) to the exact minute of legal shooting light so you'll know when it's go time. If birds land in the decoys prior to shooting time, stay still. If they stick around for a few minutes, you'll double your spread's drawing power. After the initial sunrise flurry, it's essential to find every cripple you can. Know what's in the bag so that you'll be clear on what remains of your limit.

WAIT IT OUT Some of my favorite beaver ponds are resting sites and don't come alive until long past dawn. Plan ahead to hang around for the mid-morning—or even noontime—mallard flights. Patience and discipline pay off. Try not to horse around during the slow periods, and stay an hour longer than you think you should.

TRY ONE REALLY DIRTY TRICK Beaver pond ducks are famous for landing where your decoys aren't. To keep them out of the far corners of the swamp, hang a few aluminum pie pans from low branches. Remove the scarecrows on your way out.

THE USUAL SUSPECTS

These four ducks love beaver ponds.
Here's how to bring them home.

Wood Duck Woodies aren't known to decoy easily, but they're suckers for a spinning-wing fake.

Mallard If more than two groups of greenheads snub your set for some other corner of the swamp, move immediately.

Black Duck These will circle a beaver pond, then vanish. If they drop below 35 yards, take them as they pass overhead.

Gadwall If gadwalls are in your area, toss a few gaddie decoys— or mallard hens—in a cluster near the shore side of your spread.

076 MAKE A CANOE VANISH

Floating a creek for quackers is the ultimate redneck ninja move. To make a floating island, use cable ties to attach a piece of old ladder-stand camo netting to the boat's top rails, so the material drapes down to just above the water. That'll blunt the shine on the hull from early sun. Pile up fan-shaped arrays of brush in front of the bow shooter and behind the stern seat, and set more cut brush on the gunwales. Last, extend a section of cut brush out from the boat like an outrigger just behind the center thwart on the paddling side. This hides the paddler's movements, making it easy to scull into killing range.

077 LEARN TO LOVE A SMILING MALLARD

Hollywood. Spoonbill. Bootlip. All names for the same duck: The much-maligned northern shoveler. Sure, it's got a big, fat lip designed to squeegee worms and minnows out of pond muck. Yeah, it has a sunken little chest with not much meat. But a brawny, fully plumed shoveler drake is one good-looking dude—like we all were back in the day, rocking our baby-blue prom tuxedos. So back off. And by all means eat one. It's not bad—especially with cocktail sauce.

078 HUNT YARD BIRDS

Nonmigratory flocks of giant Canada geese have become so numerous that many states have created special "resident goose" seasons—often in September—to control them. Hunting these birds is a high-odds, low-budget proposition, and a hell of a good time. Here's what to do.

FIND THE FOOD Fresh-cut cornfields and shallow mud flats with plenty of moist-soil vegetation are great places to scout. When you find birds, plan to strike fast because food sources change rapidly in September.

KEEP IT REAL Small flocks are common in September, so focus more on realism than numbers. Buy the best dozen full-bodies or shells that you can afford, and supplement them with silhouettes if need be. Place the decoys in groups of three or four around your hide, and leave plenty of room for working geese to land.

AVOID PRYING EYES Use layout blinds to keep a low profile. If you can't sit near cover, bring a spade to dig a shallow depression and further lower the blind's profile. It'll be a muddy mess, but you can use that mud to dull the shine of your blind's fabric.

CALL WITH CONFIDENCE With good decoys in the right spot, you might not need to touch a call—but don't be afraid to make some noise if it seems a flock is passing by or acting suspicious. Grab them with excited greeting calls, and finish them with soft clucks and moans as they set their wings to land.

SHOOT THE CHEEKS A 15-pound goose is tough. Think like a turkey hunter and shoot for the head. Let the birds get plenty close, then take an extra second to focus on a white cheek patch before pulling the trigger. The result will usually be a clean kill.

HELL, I CAN CLEAN THAT!

DUCK

Most folks breast out a duck because it's quick and easy, and they'd rather palpate a herd of cows than pluck a whole duck. But here's a quick and easy way to cut up waterfowl and keep the breast, leg, and thigh together, along with all that delicious fat and skin. I'm tipping my Mountie cap to ultimate Canadian redneck Brad Fenson for this one. A fellow *Field & Stream* writer, Fenson shoots about 8 tons of Alberta big game a year, but his slick method for carving up a duck is a game changer.

STEP 1 Pluck the entire breast as if you are going to fillet the meat, then continue plucking the legs all the way to the foot skin and around the lower back so that the breast, legs, and thighs are cleanly plucked.

STEP 2 First, free the breast fillets from the breastbone, being careful not to cut through the skin along the lower edge of the breast. Cut along the keel of the breastbone toward the ribs, under the collarbone, and down along the ribs. Stop the cut at the bottom of the breastbone, keeping the skin between breast and leg intact.

STEP 3 Break the leg at the hip to expose the ball-and-socket joint. Next, extend the cut at the bottom of the breast so that the knife slides through the ball-and-socket joint. Press the thigh open and continue cutting. The result will be a flat cut of duck: breast fillet, leg, and thigh, all attached with skin. Repeat on the other side.

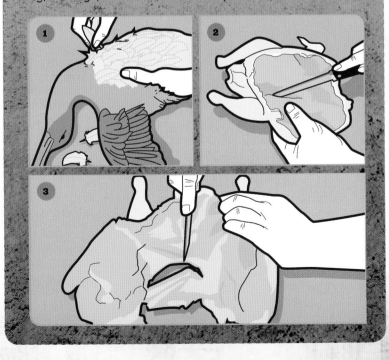

079 ROCK A PIRATE'S DUCK HEAD

Yank that sissy dream catcher off your rearview mirror and 'neck it up with this awesome DIY duck skull-and-crossbones. Your truck will gain instant swagger, as if you added a 6-inch lift.

STEP 1 Skin the upper legs and cut away most of the muscle, then skin the skull and cut out the tongue. Find a local taxidermist or nature center that will let you toss a few duck skulls and leg bones into their dermestid beetle box used to prep mounts. Well worth a $20 donation.

STEP 2 Once the bones are back from the beetles, degrease them by soaking them in warm water and Dawn dishwashing detergent for a few hours. Rinse well. Dry in the sun. To further whiten the bones, soak them overnight in hydrogen peroxide and set in the sun to dry. Use small dabs of wood glue to strengthen any loose joints. Brush bleach on stubborn brown spots, or go all natural. If you want, paint the bill yellow with acrylic paint.

STEP 3 Cross the leg bones and use a drop of hot glue to hold them in place. Once dry, build up a few layers of glue in the concave underside of the bill for a flat base, then attach the crossed bones to the back of the skull with more glue. Finish with a leather lanyard and a duck band.

WORK FOR YOUR DUCKS

We had to cross the river to get to the pothole where the teal and mallards crowded onto a 4-inch-deep puddle inaccessible by boat. But first, my buddy Lee Davis and I had to hump our mess of gear down three-quarters of a mile of railroad track and tightrope-walk across 200 yards of dark trestle. The only good thing about it was that there wasn't any hurry.

We'd started out earlier than planned. The evening before, we'd stuck the truck in the mud while scouting for ducks, so Lee called his wife to come pick us up. Thing is, we dug the wheels out before she got there. We passed Anne going in the opposite direction, and the look on her face through the driver's side window told us that heading back to the Davis house right away might not be the wise move. So we headed on down to the river and started walking.

That was with two dozen decoys on our backs, waders slung around our necks, and each of us carrying the inner tube from a dump-truck tire. We remembered the boat paddle halfway across the trestle but were too far gone by then to turn around. We sat in the tubes and used a stick to paddle ourselves across the river, which took a while. But, as it turned out, if we hadn't gotten stuck in the mud the night before, and pissed off Lee's wife, and left early for the river, we never would've made it to the ducks by shooting light. God looks out for fools and rednecks.

And he must have a particularly soft spot for good old boys just barely getting by. During college, my mode of transportation was a 1973 two-door Mercury Capri I'd bought for $300, which was all the money I had in the world. Not exactly a redneck ride, but I made do. During trapping season, I hauled beaver traps in the back seat and beaver carcasses in the trunk. During duck season we stuffed that $300 clunker with decoys and waders, laid the quilt my aunt made me as a college send-off gift across the roof, and lashed the canoe down with rope that we ran through both front windows. Once the boat was snugged down, the only way in or out of the car was through the windows, Dukes of Hazzard–style.

Our favorite spot was a marshy lake finger we dubbed Pinto Point, in honor of my buddy Jake Parrot's favorite duck-blind breakfast: a Thermos full of pinto beans, onions, and hot sauce that produced more dirty energy than a mountaintop coal mine. We had to drag the canoe in from the hardtop because there wasn't enough ground clearance in a fully packed Capri to make it down the dirt road. We had a single duck call between us—a Sure-Shot Yentzen—and no dog. We retrieved ducks with a fishing rod equipped with a Jitterbug. The one time the treble hooks failed to snag a downed bird, Jake swam out in his underwear to make the retrieve. It was January. The duck was a banded drake canvasback. It's on my wall today, more than 30 years later, and it's my favorite mounted critter of all time. That's because we got after them back then, made do with what we had, and worried less about charging the decoy batteries than calculating how many layers of waffle-weave cotton long johns it would take to keep a kid alive. Especially if you had to swim for the birds.—T.E.N.

SHOOT SOME VARMINTS

Varmints are the reason we have truck guns. Sure, you can set out to actually hunt the various critters we'll discuss here, but often as not, the chance to shoot a varmint is incidental to some other pursuit. And the reasons to shoot—aside from the fact that big bullfrogs and young raccoons make fine meals—are many. If left unchecked, overabundant predators will play hell on game populations and livestock; groundhogs denning underneath a barn will eventually cause it to collapse; and beavers will flood and destroy seasonal wetlands.

Shots at varmints are never taken out of spite. The quest to control these critters is an age-old struggle that rednecks secretly delight in—even if they complain about it at length. A coyote's intelligence and a beaver's resilience are traits to be revered and respected. If such critters disappeared tomorrow, the redneck life would be duller indeed. —W.B.

080 HUNT 'YOTES DURING DEER SEASON

My buddy Byron South is one of the country's best-known predator hunters, and he's a redneck just like you and me. He'd rather call coyotes in November than any other month because that time of year presents a perfect storm of conditions. There are more coyotes in the woods in late fall, pups born in the spring are being kicked out of the pack by the alpha animals then, and many of them have never heard a predator call.

The changing landscape makes the hunting easier too. If you look over a coyote turd in September or October, you'll see that it's as full of berries and persimmon seeds as it is feathers and fur. Coyotes are omnivores, but the first frosts nip much of the vegetation and soft mast that they prefer. When it gets cold, they turn their attention to heartier meals, such as rabbits in distress.

The fundamentals of a coyote calling set are the same regardless of the time of year. You have to beat their sense of smell and their eyesight. Don't walk across wide-open fields to your setup, and always approach and call into the wind. South says his two favorite cover scents are Copenhagen and gun solvent. (Don't make me beat you over the head with that joke.) "If a coyote's downwind, he can smell you. If he's upwind, he can't. Scent-control efforts don't much matter," South says.

Stick to distress calls in the fall, and when in doubt, go with rabbit sounds. Responding coyotes will frequently try to circle downwind of the call, but South says you can minimize that with constant calling. He uses an electronic caller, and once it's on he doesn't turn it off until the end of the set. He says that makes responding coyotes travel a more direct route to you. "If they do circle, it's usually because they think they should be able to see what they're hearing," he says. "That's where decoys help." —w.b.

081 MASTER THE COYOTE KISS

Veteran hunters call it the "coyote kiss," and you can use it to call just about any carnivore within 75 yards. I frequently use it when bowhunting deer to call passing predators into range. It's also an excellent coaxing call to use on bobcats hung up in the brush.

Execution is simple: Press your bottom lip—right where you'd place a good dip—against your top teeth. Leaving your upper teeth exposed, suck in air to create a loud kissing sound. Regulate the sound with your top lip to make it sound like some small critter in distress. That's it. The wider the gap between your two front teeth, the louder the noise. Lucky for us kids who never got braces, right?—w.b.

082 DIAL IN A COYOTE SHOTGUN

The first coyote I ever called up and killed fell to a 3-inch, 12-gauge No. 4 turkey load. It was a 15-yard headshot, and a .410 would've produced the same result. Since then, I've used a variety of shotshell and choke combinations on predators, including several sizes of buckshot and a few different "high performance" predator loads with shot sizes ranging from B to T. I've seen coyotes, foxes, and bobcats shot with all of that stuff on calling stands from Kentucky to Texas to Alberta.

My advice for predator hunters is this: If you're limited to one gun, use a rifle. But if you have the option, shotguns are good for hunting in thickets and for shooting predators over decoys (provided you have a buddy along with a rifle for backup). Rather than buckshot, go with smaller pellets—BBs up to T-shot—and pattern your loads through a variety of choke tubes. Such big pellets are notoriously finicky on the patterning board, as too much constriction can blow the pattern. Shooting from a bench at 40 yards, start with a factory modified choke, then tighten it down one shot at a time until you get your best result. The tightest I've gotten was with a Winchester load of lead BBs through a turkey tube; it threw a pattern dense enough to pulverize a coyote at more than 70 yards. —W.B.

083 BE A CAT CALLER

I'm not talking about standing on the sidewalk and heckling co-eds. That's terrible manners. I'm talking about calling bobcats. These shy, elusive felines are prized by most predator hunters and fur collectors. Calling them is more specialized than calling coyotes, though. Here's how it's done.

GET OFF THE BEATEN TRACK Coyotes are right at home digging in the neighbor's trash, but bobcats prefer rugged wilderness areas where they can avoid people. Look near creek drainages, cutovers, and remote, mountainous habitat.

GO LONG The first five minutes of a calling sequence are best for coyotes and foxes—but bobcats prefer to hang out in the brush and slip in slowly, like a house cat hunting birds. Most bobcat hunters sit and call for a minimum of 45 minutes per stand. Stick with the distress sounds you'd use for canines, but avoid coyote vocalizations.

HUNT IN THE DARK Hunting at night with a spotlight isn't legal everywhere, but it's especially effective for bobcats. Cats are more comfortable moving about at night, and their glowing eyes in the brush frequently give them away long before they provide a shot. —W.B.

084 ENJOY THE ROAST BEEF OF THE CREEK

Late every winter, we begin to see deep pools of standing water in the creek bottoms on our farm. Dad will don rubber knee boots, grab a pickax along with his rifle, and then go wading through the mud with a purposefulness seldom seen the rest of the year. He'll spend a day tearing out beaver dams and draining water, and then he'll exhaust an evening shooting beavers as they attempt to repair the damage. "They'll flood the whole damn bottoms if we don't stop 'em," he'll say without fail.

For as long as I've been out of diapers, we've been fighting this battle with beavers and water and mud in our bottoms. I've often wondered if the beavers become frustrated when they find we've destroyed their dams, or if they relish the task of rebuilding. It seems to be the latter. My great-uncle Doug, who once used his track hoe to free a pickup truck that was hung up in one of the very mud holes to which I'm referring, dutifully noted that the drainage would continue to be an issue in our bottoms because "it will always be low ground."

Truth is, Dad would be distraught if not for the beavers and the mud. As he's gotten older, he's been

trapping them more often than shooting them, and, on several occasions, he's celebrated his short-lived victories by skinning and cooking the beavers. Seared beaver tail is full of rich fat, and it's supposedly an haute cuisine delicacy. I've not tried it. But I do know boneless beaver meat, cooked in a Crock-Pot with gravy and vegetables, tastes a lot like greasy roast beef. Which, of course, is the best kind. Fortunately for us, there seems to be a never-ending supply of it. —W.B.

085 FIGHT A CHIGGER BITE

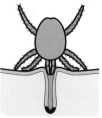

It wouldn't be so bad if chiggers roamed around solo, like an honest tick. But no, you never get just one chigger bite. You get 20, or 100, all bunched up inside the waistband of your Fruit of the Looms. The larvae of the harvest mite, it turns out, is a thigmotactic insect. That means it likes tight, cozy spaces. Once they hunker down in your butt crack, or in the cool shade of your muffin top, chiggers insert tiny mouthparts into places your mother hasn't seen since you were in diapers, inject digestive enzymes that dissolve your skin cells, then spend the next couple days sucking up the liquefied goo. Meanwhile, you're in agony. Turkey hunters tend to suffer chigger wrath more than other outdoorsmen, so here's one way to stay chigger-free: Sit on sunny rocks instead of shady logs. These little buggers can't take the heat.

086 SQUALL DOWN A COON

Traditionally, coon hunting takes place at night with hounds that run the critter up a tree, where it's either shot with a .22, shaken out of the tree and killed by the dogs, or left for another night.

You can also hunt raccoons by calling them in during their late-winter breeding season. I've had numerous coons respond to rabbit-in-distress sounds made while hunting coyotes, especially at night. For faster action, set up near a known den tree late in the afternoon, and use the "fighting coons" sound on your electronic caller.

Big male raccoons are, pound for pound, the most confrontational critters on the planet. These fighting sounds will frequently bring them on the run within seconds, so you'd best be prepared to shoot before turning on the caller.

HELL, I CAN SKIN THAT!

RATTLESNAKE

When I was growing up, my mama let my pet snakes hibernate in the family refrigerator, as long as they were tied up in pillowcases and stuffed into the vegetable crisper. Their survival rate was slightly south of 100 percent, so I learned how to skin serpents and preserve the hides early on in life. Be aware that many state laws protect snakes, so make sure you're in the clear before you set out to make your own hatband. And if you're working with a venomous serpent, make darn sure the snake is dead. Like, dead yesterday.

STEP 1 Lay the snake out on waxed paper (newspaper will turn into a slimy glop). Cut the head off cleanly with a hatchet or sharp knife. Starting at the anal vent, slit the belly all the way up to the neck.

STEP 2 Work a knife tip between the skin and meat at the neck, then work your way around the body toward the tail. Go a few inches at a time.

STEP 3 When you reach the anal vent, be careful not to tear the hide near the tail, especially if you want to retain a snake's rattles. Cut through the last few vertebrae, and scrape as much meat away from the bone as you can.

STEP 4 Use a spoon or the back of a knife to scrape any remaining flesh away from the skin. Wash it in cold water and tack it to a board. Rub salt or 5 Mule Borax into the skin, and set it in bright sun for a few days. —T.E.N.

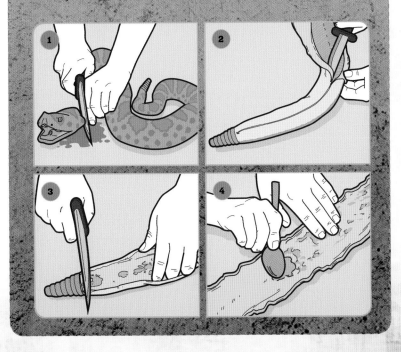

087 SHOOT FROM A TRUCK HOOD

As a youngster I learned to shoot a rifle with my daddy's friend, Keith Gleason, sniping groundhogs across cow pastures along the New River in North Carolina. We'd pull into a field, prop sandbags on the hood of Keith's truck, and start dialing in his .22-250 VarmintMaster. Keith was fresh out of the Marine Corps, and he didn't take too many shortcuts. If you missed, too bad. You had to give up the gun. I learned to miss as infrequently as possible.

There are a few really stupid and dangerous ways to shoot across the hood of a vehicle. The blowback from big rifles, especially ones with ported barrels, can crack a windshield. And if your rifle is sitting too low, then the shockwaves from a high-powered load traveling 6 inches above metal can still ripple a hood.

To safely use your rig as a tetrapod, always shoot across a corner of the hood so that the muzzle extends over the edge of the truck. Place sandbags under the rifle's fore-end and the buttstock to absorb hood flex from the recoil. Lean into the truck for stability, and fire. Just make sure that your ejected shells don't ping the windshield or drop into the engine compartment. —T.E.N.

TAKE A KID FROG GIGGIN'

You can't fake this. When you go frogging, you go all in. No messing around. There will be dirt under your fingernails—as well as muck, slime, blood, and guts. Darkness, mosquitoes, spiders in the boat, snakes hanging from low branches, DEET running into your eyes. It all just adds to the awesome.

Jack is in the front of the canoe with a headlamp and a 12-foot gig we made from bamboo growing along the creek in the backyard. I paddle with easy, quiet strokes, sweeping a spotlight along the shoreline. Hundreds of spider eyes reflect the light like green constellations. Water striders scatter. There's a muskrat. Couple snakes. And then a pair of yellow beads, unblinking, above the frowny chin of a frog.

"There he is." I don't have to say much.

"Got him," Jack replies.

I ease the boat close, careful not to rock the canoe. Nothing makes a grunt bunny more nervous than ripples from a boat. Twenty feet. Ten. Jack raises the gig like a javelin thrower.

The canoe bucks as he drives the gig down into the muck. "Easy, big man!" I shout. "Watch your balance!" He holds the gig pole with one hand, the gunwale with another.

"Get him?"

"I think so."

"Well. You know how to find out."

Stick a frog in soft mud and you've only just begun. You don't really know if there's a frog at the end of the gig or just a wad of frogless muck, because you had to jab him good and hard to drive the gig prongs through swamp water and lily pads and whatever else was out there in the dark. And maybe you missed and maybe you didn't, and if you do have him, then he's pinned down deep in the slop.

Jack slips out of the boat, keeping pressure on the gig, and squares up to the task at hand. He pulls off the headlamp and tosses it into the canoe. He slides one hand down the bamboo pole and into the water so deep that his face is barely an inch from the surface. He grimaces. This part is no fun. Then, in the glare of my own headlamp, I see him grin.

"Yessss," he hisses, like the serpent Kaa from *The Jungle Book*. He pulls the gig up and out of the water, swamp muck pouring off his arm. At the end of the gig is a mass of mud, half-decayed leaves, lily pad roots, leeches, gig tines, fingers, and frog legs. "Yes," Jack says again, as he works his hand around the frog, wrenches it off the gig, and hands it over.

I smack the frog against the canoe gunwale and drop it into a grimy pillowcase. It thumps for a few seconds, then stills. It's hardly a Boone & Crockett bullfrog, but no matter. It's an hour past sundown on a dark-of-the-moon summer night. My 11-year-old son is chest deep in a black-dark swamp, gigging frogs and happy as a clam. There'll be plenty of time for bigger game. For now, I keep paddling as he slips the headlamp back on and picks up the gig.

"Find me one, Daddy," he calls in the dark.

Must be doing something right.—T.E.N.

FISHING

Nate Hagen was feeling the pressure. It was 6:29 a.m., and in less than 60 seconds the Montauk State Park trout siren would sound. A small-town preacher from Illinois, Hagen wore shower shoes and a sleeveless T-shirt. His wife, Vicki, and three sons–all under the age of 10–had taken up a coveted position at the Social Hole, a slick, mossy pool just a few hundred feet from where the Current River bubbles out of the Missouri ground.

"Calm down, honey," Vicki said. She sat in a camp chair surrounded by Little Tikes fishing rods, boxes of Little Debbie Nutty Bars, and a block of Velveeta. Strips of white-bread crusts were piled at her feet. Vicki's mama had cut off the crusts for her Velveeta cheeseball baits when she was a girl, she told me, so it was only fitting that she extended the favor to her boys.

When the trout siren screamed, the Hagen family launched into action.

"Go, go, go!" Nate hollered to his kids. He was like Santa Claus whipping his reindeer into the sky.

"Watch your bobber, Patrick!"

"Jarrett, you got one! Pull, buddy, pull!"

"Vicki! Patrick needs more cheese!"

The feed was on, and then things got more than a little crazy. The Social Hole is known for combat fishing. The state-record brown trout was caught here, a 16-pound 12-ounce glutton that fell to a green bean.

"It's like a big cheese-and-corn casserole flowin' through the woods," one old-timer warned me just a few days before my trip. "Wear a helmet."

"We scratch some money together and come down for a week each year," Hagen said, reaching over to help 2-year-old Brandt hold on to a Finding Nemo fishing rod. "We camp right here, and hit 'er hard. We're on the water from siren to siren unless we're eating lunch."

It was only later, after the cheese froth had died off, that I rigged up my own rod for a go. Preacher Nate wandered over for a chat.

"Fishing is Biblical, you know," he said. "First thing Jesus ate after He arose from the dead was broiled fish. Book of John, I believe."

It's a gently delivered bit of the Gospel, but here at the Social Hole, Hagen had no intention of a hard sell. "At some point, though, God invented beer batter," he grinned. "And nothing's been the same ever since." —T.E.N.

PANFISH

What's in a name? As it turns out, a whole lot more than you'd think. "Panfish" is a catchall term for a whole bunch of fish species that seem to be designed for the frying pan. They're broad from top to bottom, which makes them easy to flip with a fork, but flat enough so that four minutes of frying per side is just about right. The group includes the entirety of the beloved bream family—bluegill, shellcracker, redbreast sunfish, green-eared sunfish, warmouth, and more—plus crappie and the various perches. Panfish are everywhere: in ponds, rivers, lakes, swamps, and creeks you can bound across. Most likely, your very first fish was a panfish. If you're lucky (and smart), you never quit fishing for them. A panfish might fit in a small skillet, but all those memories of tossing popping bugs to bream beds, fishing till the lightning bugs came out, and riding back to the truck on your daddy's shoulders, well, those are bigger than life. —T.E.N.

088 PULL THE LONG LINES

When the water temperature creeps above 60 degrees and spawning fish begin to scatter, a switch in tactics is in order. Like spider rigging, long-line trolling is an effective way to present multiple crappie lures—but it's a much faster way of covering water for aggressive fish.

RIG OUT THE REAR END I like to use four 8-foot, medium-action spinning rods fished directly off the stern of the boat in rod holders set to keep the rod tips at about 45 degrees. Each reel is spooled with 6-pound-test line, which I tip with a $\frac{1}{8}$-ounce crappie jig—about the right weight for fishing 10 to 12 feet of water. If I'm fishing shallower than 10 feet, I'll downsize to a $\frac{1}{16}$-ounce jig. Deeper than 15, and I'll move up to a quarter ounce. I tip my jigs with an assortment of curly and paddle-tail jig bodies in a variety of colors.

HUM IT OUT THERE A decent breeze, say 5 to 10 mph, helps keep the boat moving at about the right speed, but I use a hand-controlled trolling motor hooked to the transom to keep the boat straight. You don't want to drift any faster than 2 mph, so on especially windy days a drift sock might be needed to slow things down. Set the boat on course for your drift and then, once you're moving, fire a long cast with each rod. Flip the bails, set the rods in the holders, and have yourself a cold beer.

Expect some dead time during the drift, followed by flurries of bites when you encounter a school of fish. Be prepared to kick a buoy over the side or punch in waypoints on a GPS so that you can turn around and make repeated drifts through the best areas.—W.B.

089 FIGHT 'EM TIGHT

Crappies have wimpy fighting reputations, but the big 'uns are notorious for throwing the hook. "They don't have fingers, hands, or feet. When he moves the line, the jig is in his mouth," says Kentucky crappie guide Jack Canady. "Get the hook set immediately, and do not drop the rod tip. Keep pressure on him all the way to the net. I've seen so many monster slabs lost right at the boat when a client gets excited and lowers that rod tip. Their mouths are so soft that the jig falls right out."

090 CATCH BIG GIRLS WITH A SPIDER RIG

Few methods are more effective on offshore crappies than spider rigging. This slow-trolling tactic employs an arsenal of long rods to present multiple jigs at once. Even though it's a killer technique for fishing brush piles, veteran Kentucky Lake guide Jack Canady also uses it for catching big prespawn females suspended in open water. Here's how to make use of it.

HIT THE HIGHWAYS In late February and March, Canady fishes creek-channel edges near the major spawning flats, where 2-pound slabs are fairly common. "Prespawn females will treat those creek drops just like a bend in the road," he says. "They concentrate there in huge numbers, just waiting on the signal to move up shallow and begin spawning."

He begins early in the morning by following the contours with his side-scan unit. "Staging fish are usually suspended," he says. "Twelve feet is about the average water depth you're fishing, but the biting fish may only be 5 feet down. It's better to fish too shallow than too deep. Crappies will readily rise to hit a jig, but they'll never go down for it."

USE THE RIGHT RIG Canady's spread consists of eight 12-foot poles in rod holders on the bow of his boat. They're spooled with 6- to 12-pound monofilament. He clamps a 3/8-ounce split shot (heavier for deeper water) 18 inches above a 1/16-ounce jig secured to the line with a loop knot. Your lines must stay vertical. If they're swinging back under the boat, increase your sinker size.

BE COLORFUL Canady keeps a varied assortment of jig body colors in the water—and he's continually

experimenting with new colors throughout the day. "They'll change on a dime," he says. "They'll lock onto one color for a while, and then suddenly decide they want something different. It's important to constantly try new colors to keep them biting."

091 KICK IT WITH SWIMBAITS

Swimbaits are mainstay "kicker fish" lures for tournament bass pros, but everybody likes to catch a big one now and again, crappie fishermen included.

When I'm crappie fishing, I always have a 2-inch swimbait, like a Storm WildEye swim shad or Creme spoiler shad, rigged and handy. Trolled on 6-pound monofilament, they run 7 to 10 feet deep at crappie speeds of 1 to 1.5 mph, and they'll run deeper if you add a split shot or two. You can use them for casting the banks too, by making long throws and slow, steady

retrieves. Swimbaits rarely get big numbers of bites, but when they do get bit, it's often a slab. They've accounted for more 2-pound-plus crappies for me than everything else combined. —W.B.

092 MAKE A CRAPPIE LOVE NEST

Staking out a few crappie trees is about the best way we know of to tip the scales in your favor come crappie season. The PVC trunk and branches of this DIY tree provide perfect cover, and the slick pipes won't grab hooks and jigheads.

STEP 1 Drill a small hole through one end of a 4-inch PVC pipe. This pipe will serve as the tree's trunk. (The overall length of the pipe will depend somewhat on the depth of its final destination, but a 4- to 5-foot-tall tree usually works well.)

STEP 2 To anchor the 4-inch pipe, first insert a long nail through the small hole at the bottom of it, then set it in a 3-gallon plastic flower pot with concrete.

STEP 3 Cut six 3-foot-long sections of ¾-inch pipe (your branches), and drill a small hole through one end of two of them.

STEP 4 Drill six ¾-inch holes up and down the trunk. Make the holes so that your branches will all angle upward and shed any hooks easily.

STEP 5 Insert your ¾-inch PVC branches through the holes in the trunk and secure them with PVC glue.

STEP 6 Drill small holes in a couple of 20-ounce water bottles, fill the bottles with dry dog food, and cap them tightly. Tie these to the tree branches that have the small holes.

STEP 7 PVC doesn't register on many fish finders, so mark your trees with a GPS to keep your honeyhole a secret. If you want the tree to show up on a fish finder, drill a few holes in the top and string a few metal washers to the tree, or use pieces of bamboo as the tree branches.

093 HOLD THE MINNOWS

Small minnows are mainstay crappie baits, but they're notorious for slipping off the barb of the hook, especially when hooked through the eye sockets. One good way to hang on to your bait a little longer is by using a segment from a soft-plastic curly-tail grub as a baitkeeper. Simply snip off a pencil-eraser-size piece of the grub's body with your teeth. After securing the minnow to the hook, thread the plastic piece onto the barb, and slide it down the bend of the hook to hold the minnow in place.

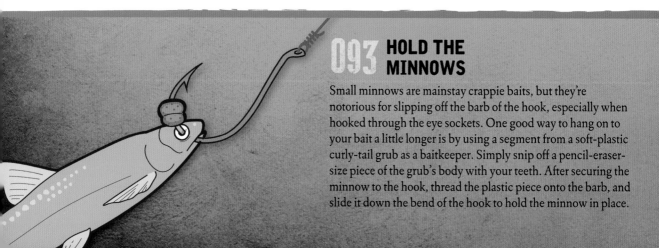

WHAT THE #*&! IS A
SAC-A-LAIT

Sac-a-lait is the Cajun word for white crappie. In French, it means "sack of milk," and some Louisianans claim that's a reference to the crappie's soft, white fillets. Others say the name comes from the Choctaw word *sakli*, which means trout. Regardless of the true origin, tell a Cajun you're headed to the bayou to catch sac-a-lait for po' boys, and he'll know what you mean.

094 KEEP A WORM BED

Summer is the season for last-minute, lazy-man, spur-of-the-moment worm drowning, so the last thing you want to do is waste serious fishing time scrounging for bait. Tuck a worm bed in between the butter beans and the zinnias—fancy-pants city folks call this *vermicomposting*—and you'll be ready to roll at the first sign the shift boss is sneaking off to the golf course.

This is basic country-boy engineering. Choose a shady spot, and build a bathtub-shaped bed out of cinder blocks. Line it with landscape plastic. Fill it half full with soaking-wet strips of newspaper and cardboard, a few shovelfuls of manure, and a couple gallons of good soil. Mix well, adding a bit more water so that the matrix is moist but not soggy. Cover the worm box with a plywood top or heavy blanket. Let it sit for a week to allow normal decomposition to take place.

Next, add a few hundred worms and feed your babies two or three times a week—lettuce, banana peels, apple cores, other veggie refuse, and the occasional treat of nongreasy leftovers are perfect. Keep the soil moist. When temperatures peak in summer, fill a milk carton with ice cubes and push it into the middle of the bedding. That makes it easier to harvest a big handful of bait too, as the worms will chill out in the cool soil.

Buddy, you are now a worm farmer. Who knows? You might even qualify for a federal agriculture subsidy.

095 GO TO BED

The search for beds is the most difficult part of bream fishing. They're pretty easy to locate in a pond or small lake, but there's an art—and maybe a little science—to it on larger bodies of water. Bream require a bottom composition soft enough for

fanning their bowl-shaped nests but firm enough that the nests won't wash away. Sand and pea-gravel banks are ideal places to look. Typically, bream beds will be in a protected pocket not far from some subtle change in depth, like a creek channel or a shallow ditch. Early in the season, nests might be in 10 inches of water, but the most productive beds are usually 4 to 6 feet deep. Shellcrackers frequently nest a bit deeper. I've found their beds in 10 feet of water.

096 MAKE A BREAM PEE

At the peak of the spawning season, male bluegills are full to the gills (pun intended) of milt. A gentle squeeze of the fish's belly will expel a stream of it out to a good 3 or 4 feet, and there's not one single redneck kid alive who won't think a "peeing" fish is one of the most hilarious things that they've ever seen.

097 'CRACKER THE CODE

Though a bobber-and-bait will catch plenty of bluegills, a slightly more specialized rig helps when you're after redear sunfish, a.k.a. "shellcrackers." These prized southern panfish are hard fighters, and they frequently grow to 2-plus pounds. But they mostly eat mollusks and snails—hence the nickname—and don't rise far off bottom to feed. That's why a drop-shot rig makes a lot of sense for catching them.

My favorite version consists of a ¼-ounce bell sinker with a 4-inch dropper loop tied into the line about a foot above the weight. Simply pull that loop through the eye of your hook, pull the hook through the tag-end loop, and cinch it tight. This allows your bait to flutter just off bottom as you drag the weight along. With a 7½-foot

medium-action spinning rod, you can cast it a country mile, which makes it great for covering water. When in search mode, I sometimes substitute the hook and live bait with a tiny jig so I'm not constantly rebaiting my hook.

Once I find a bed of fish, I switch to a long-shank hook and redworms (which seem to catch three times as many shellcrackers as nightcrawlers do). Toss the rig into the bed and keep your rod just high enough that the line stays tight. Reel it back slowly, with frequent 30-second pauses, and chances are you'll get a bite. Channel cats and keeper bass frequently hang around bluegill beds, and they'll hit this rig too. Both add substantial meat to the fillet pile.—w.b.

098 FISH LIKE THEY DO IN L.A. (NO, NOT THAT ONE)

Kenny Dean hails from Lower Arkansas and has been bluegill fishing in southern oxbow lakes since 1946. "The best I ever did was in a cypress swamp below Stuttgart," he says. "We caught 22 bluegills that weighed 23 pounds."

"It's easier to catch them when they're on the bed, but the fishing leading up to the spawn is when you catch the biggest ones," he says. "Bigger than your hand."

Dean's oxbow fishing techniques work anywhere big bluegills and wood cover are found. Dean runs a 15-foot johnboat with a 15-horse motor, but cypress trees call for specialized equipment. "I like a sculling paddle for this type of fishing," Dean says. "If you use a trolling motor, you'll hit the knees, break your prop, and scare the fish."

Dean uses a 10-foot-long telescoping fiberglass rod with a length of 12-pound line and no reel. Cane poles work too. "I rig two poles," he says. "One with 7 or 8 feet of line for fishing submerged logs and brush. The other just has 2 feet of line, to probe tight spots up next to the cypress knees."

The heavy line allows him to easily free the tiny hooks when they snag. (If you do this right, you'll snag them pretty darn often.)

"I tie on a small hook and sinker or a tiny jig. Early in the season, I tip it with a waxworm," Dean says. "Later in the year, I switch to crickets or redworms. The key to this is to control your drop. That bait sinks very slowly, so you have to keep your line taut and watch it constantly for a strike. Ease it down next to one piece of cover, hold it there for 20 or 30 seconds, then pull it out and drop it next to another one."

099 SHOP LOCAL

You can ask Mr. Google about fishing all you want, but he knows squat compared to the fine folks manning the Nabs rack at your local bait shop. That's how I wound up with a dozen sickly looking wet flies the locals around Fargo, Georgia called "sallies," which I was told was all I needed to load my boat with Okefenokee Swamp fliers.

Nabs Man directed me to a rack of the flies, all locally tied. They came two to a pack and were displayed on a tall wire rack that I'd bet held potato chips once the fishing slowed down. Had I been merely browsing on my own, I wouldn't have looked at them twice. Instead, I bought two dozen and fished them like the man said: on light line, under a light bobber, as close to stumps and swamp slop as I could get them.

I didn't sink the boat with fliers, but I caught them right and left, plus warmouths and even a bowfin, and fished til the sun started setting and the alligators got a little too close for comfort. It was a lesson everybody needs to relearn now and then. Don't ever drive by the bait shop that's right there at the boat ramp. There's a Nabs Man in most every one, and while Mr. Google can get you to the water, Nabs Man will get you into fish. —T.E.N.

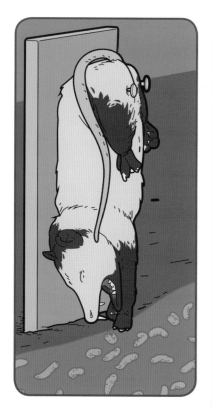

HELL, I CAN SCALE THAT!

BREAM

Why wouldn't you want succulent, boneless panfish fillets? Because the classic southern bluegill recipe calls for picking around the bones of a scaled fish fried whole, that's why. Though I love fillets, scaled bream do have a distinctive extra hint of flavor that's pretty danged tasty—plus, you can eat the fins. Here's how to get a mess of them ready for the grease.

SCALE 'EM FIRST Before removing the head, take the edge of a spoon and scrape it along the fish's side, from the tail to the pectoral fin. The scales will slide right off in clumps, leaving smooth skin underneath. Repeat on the other side.

REMOVE THE HEAD AND GUTS Take off the head with a sharp knife by cutting just behind the gill plate. Next, slice the belly open and use your fingers to scrape out any remaining guts. Bluegill heads with guts intact make fine catfish bait and excellent garden fertilizer alike.

CLIP THE DORSAL FIN While almost all of the fins are considered a delicacy when fried, the spiny dorsal fin is not. Remove it with a pair of catfish-skinning pliers. After that, wash the fish in cold water, slice up a fresh tomato, and get ready for supper.

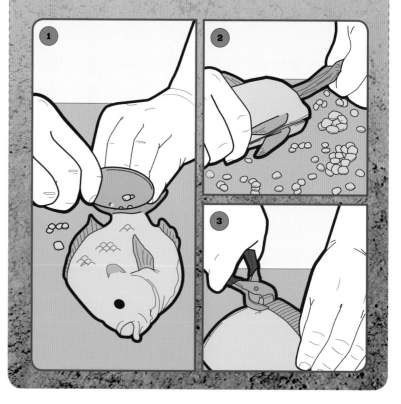

100 CHUM BREAM WITH MAGGOTS

It sounds nasty, it smells nasty, and it is nasty, but there is also no sense denying that chumming farm-pond bream with maggots is a killer tactic. Back in the day, old-timers nailed a horse head or whole possum over good water and let the flies do their tricks. In England, carp anglers hurl maggots with slingshots to chum up a good bite. A more civilized method, which is right in the wheelhouse for avid panfish anglers, is to hoist a wire basket on a pole over the water and stuff it with fish guts, heads, and filleted bodies from your last fishing trip. Maggots sink, and bream will congregate for the big feed.

102 MAKE A BLUEGILL POPPER FROM A WINE CORK

We haven't yet figured out a way to turn a twist-off Mad Dog 20/20 cap into a bona fide lure, but we're not giving up. Meanwhile, you can convert any wine cork into a fine bream popper in about five minutes flat, using materials you likely have in the house.

Use a rotary tool to shape a wine cork. With a razor blade, slice a ¼-inch-deep groove into the bottom of the cork, push the hook shaft into place, and secure it with Zap-a-Gap. Paint the cork or seal it with two-part epoxy. For the body fur, snip hair from an old deer hide. For legs, stripe pieces of a rubber band with a permanent marker. Attach legs and body fur at the base of the cork with fly-tying thread and another dab of Zap-a-Gap. That's it. Go fish.

103 FISH A CORK RIG FOR RIVER REDBREAST

"I think a worm's about the sorriest bait there is for river fish," Jim Greek once told me, and he would know. Greek, a former Florida wildlife enforcement officer, fished the Suwannee River for redbreast sunfish three days a week, 12 months a year, and almost every fish he caught ate a cricket. In a single month he certified a world-record redbelly four different times.

Greek once showed me the secret to his success, devised over decades of fishing. First, he likes as little friction as possible in his slip corks, to allow the cricket to freely bump along the bottom of a river that might vary in depth from 5 to 20 feet. To ensure that the line moves smoothly through the slip cork, Greek removes the peg from a 2-inch slip cork and pushes the plastic insert from a slip cork the next size up into the line channel. He tips the line with a No. 6 extra-light wire hook topped with a small orange bead and a ¹⁄₁₆-ounce bullet weight.

You have to be on your toes to fish the rig, but it's worth the effort. "It don't get hung up as bad, and it drifts deeper," Greek told me. "Sometimes those little differences make a big difference." Like, a world record of difference. —T.E.N.

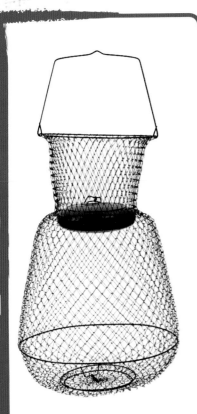

101 BE A BASKET CASE

Aerated live wells are nice, but the average aluminum bream boat doesn't have one. Besides that, bluegills in a live well tend to die quickly when it becomes crowded—which is bound to happen when you find a hot bed. For keeping your fish fresh in warm water, it's tough to beat a collapsible wire fish basket hung over the side and tied to the gunwale. With a spring-loaded, one-way door, it's faster than messing with the door on a live well—and when you're trying to outcast your wife to the best spots, speed is a good thing. At about $8 apiece, you can afford a basket for everyone in the boat.

104 SPOTLIGHT WHITE BASS

Early spring isn't the only time to load a cooler with white bass. These schooling fish roam river channel edges late in the summer, and they'll swarm to feed on schools of baitfish. Some of the best fishing for summertime whites happens late at night with the help of a submersible light.

The best lights are tube shaped with a clear plastic housing and made especially for fishing. They have a ring on the bottom for a sinker and another on the top for a line. They use long alligator clamps to connect to your boat's battery. Once submerged about 10 feet under your boat, they throw off an eerie green cone of light, which will attract baitfish—and white bass in return, which tend to hang out just underneath the food.

Assuming that using multi-hook presentations are legal in your waters, tie three or four crappie jigs into your line (with about 6 inches between each) and a vertical jig for bass in the open water. When you hook a fish, keep the line tight, but don't be in a hurry to reel in. When white bass get going, it's easy to hook multiple fish on one drop.

105 FISH THE DEPTHS FOR ELEPHANTS

In 50 years of perch fishing, Lloyd French has heard all the tricks. "Some people chum with minnows or dog food. Once I even saw a guide sink a clear plastic jug with water and minnows as a decoy," French says. "None of that works too well." But he does have his own tricks.

RUN LONG French runs 17 miles one way to get to his fishing spots on Lake Erie. Community holes closer to the ramp yield perch, but they're small. "My average perch in prespawn is 11 or 12 inches long, including some 2-pounders," French says. "But you have to run to get to them."

GO DEEP French's top spots all have one thing in common: the right depth. "The biggest perch are always 37 to 40 feet down, and you can mark them with a depth finder," he says. "They appear as small, pencil-shaped marks on the graph. If you see a few of them just off the bottom, there are probably plenty more holding around."

STRAIGHTEN UP French prefers a vertical rig with a slip sinker between two hooks—it's a little easier to hook two fish per drop with a vertical rig than with the pre-rigged perch spreaders many anglers use. "Once they turn on, the bite is fast. Usually you can hook one, give it a few seconds, and then get another one on the second hook," he says. "The key is to keep your rig on the bottom, though. White bass will hold above a school of perch. If you catch them, you've got your rig too high."

STAY NATIVE Regardless of the rig, French insists on using lively, native baitfish. "Here, Lake Erie shiners will outcatch golden shiners five to one," he says. "It may be different on the lake you're fishing."

FIRE 'EM UP Eventually, even the hottest bite slows down. "If they quit, and we need a few more to make a limit, I hook up a couple of fresh-caught perch from the live well and drop them down next to my buddy's line," French says (check local regs first). "I lift and drop them; that often gets the school fired up enough to put a few more slabs in the boat."

106 AMBUSH SPAWNING WHITE BASS

Early-spring spawning runs of huge numbers of white bass take place just about the time most of us are itching to get back outside, and it's pretty easy to get in on the fun before turkey season opens. These fish run out of big reservoirs to spawn in tributary riffles and rapids, but the trick is to catch them before they get too close to their love nests.

FIND THE CURRENT BREAK Look for places where the current eddies and slows. Both natural and man-made current breaks will hold white bass staging in the river until the water warms. Cast behind large rocks, bridge pilings, river islands, rock slides, bank cave-ins, downed trees—anything that might slow the current.

LOAD TWO RODS Fish two medium-action spinning rods—one spooled with some 8-pound monofilament for open water, and another loaded with heavier line for probing brush. Tie on a ¼-ounce jig with a curly-tail grub.

CAST AT AN ANGLE Fire your cast slightly upstream of the current break, and allow the jig to bounce along the bottom as it moves through the slack water.

GET SERIOUS ABOUT PANFISH

Ron Morris tossed a cricket through a dinner-plate-size hole in a mass of tangled vines and Spanish moss. Slender as a willow branch, bearded and baked by the sun, his friends call him "Altamaha Jones" because he knows every crooked-up side channel in this southern Georgia stream. He frowned as soon as he cast, and from the front of his boat I could read his mind: That ain't right. He raised the rod tip and wiggled the cork a few inches to the left. A swirl of river current grabbed the cork and carried the cricket into a dark corridor beyond the vines, like a toy boat in the breeze. And right there, where the grapevines shaded a maple tree, the bobber disappeared.

"There he is," Morris muttered. He hoisted a fat shellcracker over the side of his battered johnboat. "He can't hide but so long."

That man could fish, I'll tell you. I don't think I've seen his equal since. Not with a bobber and a cricket, anyway. And not when you have to sneak a hook through a hole in the brambles that a cottonmouth could hardly squeeze through. "This here is kamikaze fishing," Morris said. "Catch a fish, lose a hook, catch a fish, lose a bobber. A lot of folks can't take it."

He could. Morris ran an old johnboat with an old two-stroke motor to old fishing holes held for decades like family secrets. He and his buddy, Jason Strickland, fish hard and often. At that moment, we were anchored at a place they call "Cracker Barrel." They've fished this exact "bream drop"—their term for any spot that's worth a few casts—for better than 10 years. Strickland's daddy fished it for decades but only showed it to his son after turning his full attention to white perch. Strickland doesn't begrudge his father. "People around here are serious about their bream," he figured.

Come spring, I divide my time between turkey hunting, trout fishing, and chasing saltwater mackerel, but a man like Altamaha Jones sets his cap for a single pursuit and stays with it through thick or thin. "We're out here, fish or no fish," he said. It's a doggedness that leads to knowledge you don't get without commitment. Fish like Morris fishes and you'll know that a worm ain't just a worm—that there's a difference between a Florida pink and a red wiggler and a jumping jack and a "slop worm," which is what you dig out of the ground where you toss your old beans, leftover eggs, and whatever slop you happen to have around. And that difference can be seen on your stringer.

"Drives me crazy," Morris said. "You hear people say, 'Well, I think I'll take the kids bream fishing today.' Like that's all there is to it. Just throw your hook out there and the fish will jump on it. But that ain't how it is. Not with these river fish, anyways. You gotta want these durn bream pretty bad."

One night, as we fried fish by the river and sopped up the grease with hot biscuits, pileated woodpeckers hammered in the dark swamp woods. Morris looked across the broad expanse of river, its surface roiled with current seams and eddy lines and boils of upwelling water.

"I used to bass fish," he drawled, "but I burned out. When my boy was coming up, I'd take him and it was always: 'Sit down, shut up, don't do that, be quiet.' He quit fishing for a long time."

Morris poked at the fire. "Once I got hooked on these ol' river bream, I gave up the bass. Now, if I got a river under me, I'm happy. Sometimes, if it gets too long since I've been on moving water, I'll sit on the toilet and flush a few times. You know, just to make myself feel better."—T.E.N.

CATFISH

I don't know if it's the slime or the stink that draws rednecks to catfish. It could be their gargantuan size—and the fact that big cats regularly snack on more "proper" gamefish such as bass and crappies.

But most likely, it's just that catfish are practical. They're found in tiny ponds, big rivers, and major lakes the countryside over. They're almost always willing to bite, and you don't need anything special to catch one. A spincast combo, hook, sinker, and worm will work. So will a baited line tied to a green limb or suspended under a Clorox bottle. If you're feeling especially tough, you can run your arm under a rock and grab a catfish with your bare hands.

Catfish can be grilled, blackened, sautéed, boiled, or baked—but let's be real: They're at their best when deep-fried and served with white beans and beer. —W.B.

107 FISH THE BENDS

I was fishing the upper stretches of a Tennessee River tributary, and could hear the fight. The sounds of a strained Zebco 33 in the hands of a 12-year-old kid battling a catfish a third his size aren't subtle. I'd been catching pond-raised cats my whole life and had never seen a fish even half the size of that kid's. But no more than an hour later, I reeled up a channel cat that was even bigger.

If you want to catch a big cat, river fishing is the way to go. Spring rains and high, swift, muddy water make life difficult for sight-feeding species, but catfish love it. And it's the ideal situation for anchoring your boat on the inside of a sharp, deep stream bend and casting toward the undercut outside of the bend. The current can be stout, so use tackle that can both cast a heavy egg sinker and whip a double-digit catfish. My standard rig is a flipping stick with braided line, a heavy slip-sinker rig, and monofilament leader. Plan on snagging a lot and losing a few leaders. But you can also plan on landing some channel cats worth bragging about. —W.B.

108 LEARN TO LOVE LILY PADS

Channel catfish begin feeding heavily as soon as the water temperature tops 50 degrees in early spring. Look for them in shallow, muddy bays and ponds, as those waters will warm faster and retain heat better than clear, rocky areas. Warm-water spots are often full of dormant lily pads too. The thick roots of the pads create a maze of cover, and last year's dead lily pads cover the mud bottom with detritus that's appetizing to baitfish, invertebrates, and even the catfish themselves. I've caught big stringers of channel cats from dormant pad fields whose bulging bellies were full of plant matter.

Lily pad roots can be as big around as your arm, and even small catfish can get tangled in them. You need a flipping stick and baitcasting reel spooled with 30-pound braid, minimum. I tie on a standard slip-sinker rig with a 20-pound monofilament leader and 3/0 Kahle hook. For good numbers of fish in the early season, fresh chicken liver is tough to beat.

Good bays might only be a couple feet deep, but a subtle creek channel usually meanders through them. Catfish use those channels like highways; begin fishing around their edges. If you can reach them with a long cast from the bank, great.

You'll get more strikes if the rod is out of your shaky hands and propped against a stick on the bank. Just keep an eye out so a fish doesn't pull your rod into the water.

When you get a strike, allow the fish to pull the line taught, ease your hands onto the reel, and, when you feel tension from the fish, set the hook hard and get control of the fish fast to keep it from snagging up in the pads. —W.B.

109 CATCH CATFISH WITH LINGERIE

Doughballs are notoriously difficult to keep on a hook, but it's an easy fix if you happen to have a pantyhose fetish. First, make the bait by mixing bloody hamburger and flour; liver and dough; or hot water and cornmeal mixed with licorice and sugar. Press a bait-size ball of the mix into the toe of pantyhose, and tie off the hose with a piece of dental floss snugged down to the doughball. Now tie another piece of dental floss an inch up the hose from the first one, and snip the hose between the two floss wraps. Repeat until you have enough dough-filled hose baits to get you through the night.

110 GO NOODLING

I was still groggy when my wife chased my little brother out the front door, vowing to whip his ass with a spatula as she pursued him. It was the only weapon she could find to suit her temperament so early in the morning. To prompt such a threat, Matt had just informed Michelle—albeit reluctantly—that he had just wakened to find he'd ruined a new set of clean sheets on the guest bed with bloody smears and drips from the flathead catfish bite on his arm.

Thing is, ghat fish itself was worth any beating. It was an 80-pounder that Matt and I had wrestled from underneath a shallow rock at the mouth of the river just the day before. It took the two of us to lift the thrashing behemoth out of the water for a photo opportunity, and only after we released it did Matt realize he was bleeding from a good set of toothy bite marks up his arm.

We caught that fish four summers ago, and it's still been the biggest flathead that we've ever encountered. If you decide you want to go about noodling the right way, be sure to keep in mind that you're going to end up cut, beaten, and bruised. Maybe even whipped with a spatula. But you'll also catch the biggest catfish of your life, and certainly pad your redneck résumé.—W.B.

111 LEARN SOME WRASSLIN' MOVES

I've seen 12-year-olds who wouldn't watch a bobber for 5 minutes take to grabbing catfish as if it were the secret to an eternal summer break. You don't have to be a bodybuilder to do this, either. Physical strength doesn't hurt, but proper technique, a love of being in the water, and a taste for some mild violence are all far more important when you're wrestling catfish.

Catfish fight with their heads and tails. Subdue both ends and you can often noodle a flathead without suffering more than a scratch or two. If the tail gets away from you, the fish will peel the skin off your arm all the way to the boat. If you let go of the head, you'll have to explain to your buddies why you lost the fish, which is worse than any physical harm you might endure.

STEP 1 When you get a fish, grab its lower jaw and pin the fish to the bottom, to keep it from rolling.

STEP 2 Slip your other hand underneath the gill plate, being careful not to damage the gills.

STEP 3 Ease the fish out of the hole and pull its chin tight against your chest.

STEP 4 As the tail comes out of the hole, wrap your knees around the fish's midsection and cross your ankles. Its tail will fan between your calves—far better than thrashing your arm in open water.

STEP 5 Have a buddy pull you to the bank or boat, and break out the stringer.—W.B.

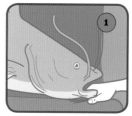

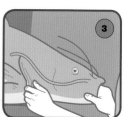

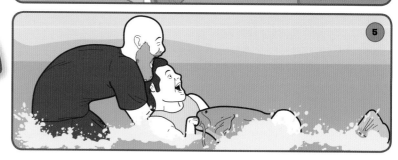

112 GET THE HOTS FOR CATS

Despite it being her third trimester, Michelle wouldn't hear of being left at home. Her very pregnant belly looked like a slider turtle as she bobbed around in the lake on her back. You could fry an egg on the deck of my boat as we wrangled some big catfish. Three days later, on June 19, our son was born.

This story is a reference for knowing when it's time to go noodling. Things don't get good until the water temperature hits 80-plus degrees. That's the trigger that puts flatheads on the nest, and it takes a stretch of blistering summer heat to get there. Our season in

Kentucky opens June 1; the best fishing often won't happen for a couple of weeks around my boy's birthday.

Channel cats, blues, and flatheads spawn in underwater holes and cavities—under a boat ramp, a rock pile, a logjam, or a washed-out bank beneath the roots of a tree. Early in the spawn, it's common to find two fish in one hole, but the females leave shortly after, leaving the males to hang back and defend the nest. The idea is to run your arm inside that hole, wiggle your fingers in front of an ill-tempered flathead's face, and wait for it to swallow your hand. Then the fight begins. —W.B.

113 SPEAK THE LOCAL LINGO

My first noodling trip took place in Greenwood, Mississippi, where they call it hand-grabbin'. When I said I was excited about going "noodling," they called me a Yankee and threatened to leave me on the bank. I've also heard it called grabbling, tickling, hogging, stumping, snatching, and simply hand-fishing. If you happen to be an out-of-state noodling guest, knowing the local lingo is second in importance only to knowing the local regulations, since being called a Yankee is almost as bad as getting a ticket. —W.B.

114 GET THE GEAR

There's a virtually standard set of things you should be wearing and bringing with you when you go noodling. Here are the most important ones.

SLEEVELESS T-SHIRT For some reason, all noodlers feel compelled to cut the sleeves off their favorite T-shirts. If you seek acceptance, you'd best do the same.

DO-RAG Keeps the top of your head from getting burned. I opt for camo, but anything with skulls, fire, and/or barbecue advertisements is okay.

ROPE STRINGER The live well on your fancy bass boat ain't big enough for the fish you'll be catching.

FLY ROD These are perfect for whipping a reluctant first-timer right out of the boat.

GARDENING GLOVES Give your mitts a little protection from a thrashing cat's jaws.

RIVER SHOES You find cat holes with your feet. Old tennis shoes offer the illusion of protection from alligator snappers. —W.B.

115 GET THE LOW DOWN

Got questions about noodling? Well, luckily for you, we have plenty of answers.

AREN'T THERE SNAKES DOWN THERE? Snakes have to breathe air, so there aren't really any under the water. But that's a giant cottonmouth on the bank right over there.

DOES A CATFISH BITE HURT? No more than laying your bare arm against a belt sander.

WHAT SCARES A NOODLER MOST? I'd say crankbaits, since flatheads sometimes steal them from bass fishermen and then carry them around stuck in their mouths for a while.

WHAT'S THE BIGGEST FLATHEAD YOU'VE EVER SEEN CAUGHT? My brother's 80-pounder. A buddy of mine in Mississippi caught and weighed a 98-pounder, but I didn't see it.

HOW DO YOU HOLD YOUR BREATH THAT LONG? Practice in the bathtub.

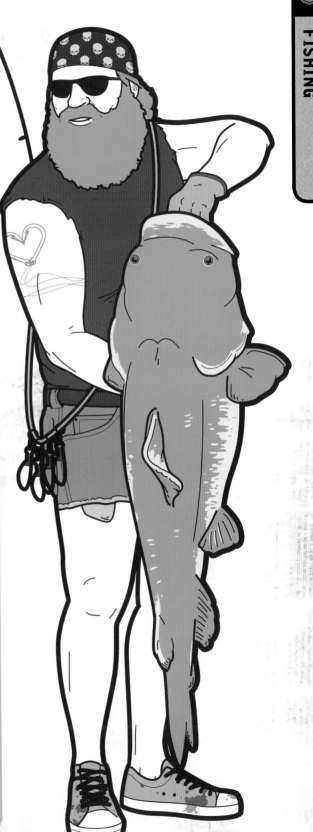

116

MAKE A SURVIVAL BUSH HOOK

Every redneck thinks that he could survive the zombie apocalypse with little more than a pocketknife and his woods smarts, snaring squirrels and spearing rabbits. Trigger snares are super survival tools, but when chosing your prey, remember that there are a lot more bluegills and catfish than tree rats, and they make for much easier pickings.

STEP 1 Find a sapling near the edge of the water. Look for places where fish congregate—deep holes on the outside of streambeds or trees that have fallen into the water.

STEP 2 Carve a simple trigger, comprising a base and a hook with a notch cut into each one as shown. Tension from the bent sapling will keep the trigger "cocked" until a fish takes the bait, tripping the trigger and snapping the sapling upright.

STEP 3 Tie a cord from the top of the sapling to the top of the trigger hook. Tie a fishhook to one end of a length of fishing line and bait it.

STEP 4 Tie the other end of this line to the bottom of the trigger hook, where the two notches fit together. Bend the sapling over so that the trigger hook points down—and that's where you pound the trigger base into the ground.

STEP 5 Set the snare by fitting the notches together, and place the baited hook in the water.

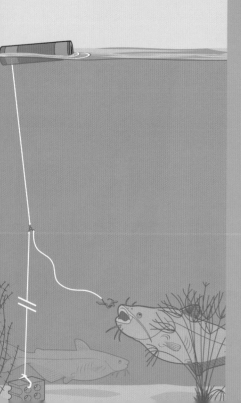

117 MAKE A POOL NOODLE JUGLINE

Nothing says summer like chasing down catfish jugs gone wild. Here's a way to recycle foam pool noodles into killer jugs. Follow these instructions and you'll be able to fit five of them upright in a 5-gallon bucket. (Be sure to check your local laws. Some areas require identification on juglines.)

STEP 1 Cut a 5-foot pool noodle into 1-foot sections. Wrap one end of each section with duct tape to protect the noodle from line cuts. Next, use a large darning needle or crochet hook to string a 4-foot length of stout 60- to 80-pound monofilament or trotline cord through the noodle above the tape. Tie one end to a washer or bead, and pull it snug against the noodle; then, tie a three-way swivel to the other end.

STEP 2 Attach 20- to 40-pound monofilament to the lower ring of the three-way swivel; use enough to reach the bottom. Anchor this with enough weight for the current. To the other ring, tie on a 4-foot dropper line of 20-pound fluorocarbon and a circle hook. Reduce line twist as you wrap line around the noodle for storage with a barrel swivel near the weight. If you're fishing at night, wrap some reflective tape around the other end.

STEP 3 Bait the hooks with small live bluegills, wads of nightcrawlers, or cut bait.

118
CHUM FOR POND CATS

If you're squeamish about grinding baitfish up in the kitchen blender, then maybe you're not the catfish hunter you think you are. There's a seemingly endless list of great ideas for catfish chum, from the relatively sanitary (dried dog food or range cubes scattered along the pond edge) to the downright nasty (fetid bluegills pureed in your blender and then frozen into blocks).

They all work the same way: by drawing cats to your fishing grounds. The trick is to get the fish hangry—hungry and angry—by stoking their appetites without letting them fill their bellies. Just stuff an onion sack or burlap bag with your chum of choice, toss in a few rocks so it will sink, tie it off, and toss it in the water. Make sure to attach a line to the chum bag so you can retrieve it later.

HELL, I CAN SKIN THAT!
CATFISH

Your garage or tool shed should hold everything you need to skin a catfish. If it doesn't, you need to quit cleaning it out so often. Start with a 3-foot length of 2x6, untreated if possible. Place the board on a level, waist-high surface—such as a truck tailgate—and get cracking.

STEP 1 Use a sharp knife to score the skin around the head in front of the gill plates. Make another slit down the back to the tail. Drive a nail through the fish's skull and into the board. Cut off the dorsal fin.

STEP 2 Brace the board against your waist with the fish's tail near your body. Grasp the skin with pliers and peel it back toward the tail. The skin may come off whole or in several strips.

STEP 3 Remove the fish from the board, grasp the head in one hand and the body in the other, and bend the head down sharply to break the spine. Bend the body up and twist to separate the head from the body. Most of the guts will come out with the head, but be sure to split the belly open and clean out any that remain inside.

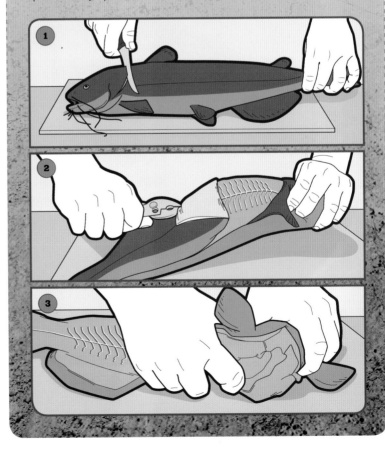

119 EAT A CAT BELLY

Outside of the bones and guts, you can eat near everything on a flathead catfish. The fillets are choice, but the belly meat is even better. Cut it off in a boneless slab, trim away the membranes, and then slice it into long, finger-diameter strips. However you cook it, it's wild, mild, and tasty.

Flatheads also have two big hunks of meat extending from behind their eyeballs down to their cheeks. Removing that is easiest if you first make a pilot cut, then pull the skin away with pliers. That exposes the meat, which you can then separate from the skull. The cheeks are a little tougher and chewier than the fillets or belly meat—but delicious nonetheless.

WHAT THE #*&! IS A

FIDDLER

Order some fried catfish in a decent southern restaurant, and you'll have the choice between boneless fillets and fiddlers. Fiddlers are simply bone-in channel cats of about 2 pounds, skinned, gutted, and with the heads removed. Like whole fried bream, the bones and fins add extra flavor that's well worth preserving if you appreciate good fried fish.

120 MAKE GLOWING LIMBLINES

My fishing buddy Will Robey is about as proud of his redneck heritage as anyone, and he came up with a glowing limbline design that's useful, cheap, and fun— which is really all a redneck needs to hear before breaking out the wallet. Here's what you need to build glowing lines of your own.

BRAIDED TROTLINE CORD Buy it in the 200- to 300-pound-test range. Larger than that and it's difficult to thread through the eyes of your hooks. You can use tarred line (which seems to hold up longer) or non-tarred line. I can't tell that it makes any difference to the fish.

HEAVY BARREL SWIVELS Big channel catfish roll when hooked. A heavy barrel swivel tied into the line a couple feet or so above the hook keeps the limbline from twisting.

EGG SINKERS A sinker keeps live baitfish from swimming out of the strike zone. In light current, 2-ounce weights are plenty. You may need to go with 6 ounces or more in swifter rivers and streams.

TRAILER REFLECTORS Stick-on trailer reflectors serve double duty. They provide a convenient place for writing your name, address, and phone number (a legal requirement for limblines in most places), and they allow you to check your lines at night from a distance with a flashlight. There's no question of whether you've "got one" with these reflectors on your line.

HEAVY HOOKS Kahle, Octopus, and standard J-style hooks all work, but use a 6/0 hook, minimum. Time and again, straightened hooks have proven to me that they're the weak link in a limbline. Bait them with live baitfish or fresh cut bait, and hang them on springy, green limbs bigger around than your thumb but smaller than your wrist. Once your lines are set, it's a simple matter of sitting back and waiting for a mess of cats to take the bait. —W.B.

121 CATCH LIVE BAIT WITH YOUR HANDS

You don't have 10 fingers (give or take) for nothing: The best baits out there are yours for the taking.

THE BAIT	HOW TO CATCH IT	HOW TO FISH IT
HELLGRAMMITE The larvae of the dobsonfly looks like something that crawled out of a zombie's eye socket. It might give you the heebie-jeebies, but it catches trout and smallmouth bass like crazy.	Pin the creature to a rock or stream bottom with firm pressure on the hard collar behind its head. Then, slowly slide your thumb and forefinger down the sides of the collar, pinch, and pull it up. Ignore the hellgrammite's tail—it's the pincers you need to worry about.	Run a light wire hook under and out the collar behind its head. Fish it with just enough weight to bump it along the bottom in broken riffle water.
GRUBS These small cylinders of white bug goo might look like sacks of snot, but the larvae of various beetles are candy to panfish and trout.	Make like a grizzly bear and turn over rotting logs. Scrape away the bark and poke into soft wood to reveal the grubs.	Tip a $\frac{1}{64}$ or $\frac{1}{128}$ jighead with a grub and you'll be a crappie king. Carolina rigs are deadly too, if you fish a search rig.
CRAYFISH You know what they are and how good they are for catching fish. You just have to get over yourself and grab the dang things.	If you can't bring yourself to reach out and grab a crawdad, try this method: With palms down and fingers outstretched, place your hands on either side of a likely-looking rock. Move your hands together under the rock, then scoop up a double handful of muck, sand, and, hopefully, a crayfish.	Insert a hook through its tail a half inch from the end to allow the crawdad to move naturally. In streams with lots of rocks, try hooking them sideways through the "horn" on the head to keep them from scooching under stones.
TIGER BEETLE LARVAE Those pencil-eraser-sized holes in the bare spots of your front yard are the burrows of tiger beetle larvae, which fish love. And they make for a good excuse to keep a sorry yard too.	Pick a slender, straw-like stem of grass about 10 inches long. Drop it gently into the hole, until you feel it bump against the larva's noggin. Wait until you see the stem twitch, a sign that the creature is pissed off enough to try to move the grass with its pincers. Yank it out in one quick snatch.	A tiger beetle baby suddenly yanked out of the crib is not a happy bug. Pinch the head off so it can't pinch back, and thread it on a hook like you would any other grub.
CATALPA WORMS Every redneck kid knows catalpa worms are like crack to bluegills and catfish. The caterpillar of the catalpa sphinx moth feeds only on the leaves of catalpa trees. Find one worm and you've found a gazillion.	The caterpillars are harmless. Pick them off one by one, or spread out a tarp or towel and shake them loose by the coffee-can full. Store in the fridge in a ventilated container, or freeze with cornmeal in a zippered freezer bag.	Turn a catalpa worm inside out to supercharge the bite. Cut the head off and use a small stick to push the body through the tough skin. Be strong—that oozing green slime is nature's chum.
CICADAS There are two kinds: the "periodical" cicadas that come out every 13 or 17 years, and the "dog-day" cicadas you can find every summer. Either one works great for bass, catfish, and bream with a big appetite.	Cicadas are as fat as pigs-in-a-blanket, but they can't bite, so just pluck them off the branches where you find them. Don't look them in their huge red eyes, though, as that will hypnotize most people.	Float a live cicada on top of the water with a light bobber. The big wings will give it a buzzbait ruckus. Sink dead cicadas into catfish country with split shot.

122 BAG BAIT IN BULK

If you just can't bring yourself to go one-on-one with a creek lobster, there are other ways to fill a bait bucket. But don't think you're going to win style points by doing any of the following.

GET YOUR KICKS Seining up a mess of local live bait will help put fish in the creel in a jiffy, and this packable kick seine folds up small enough to stow in a vest pocket or tackle bag. Sew a sleeve into the short sides of a 30x12-inch piece of white, flexible nylon netting, screen, or mesh. Use nylon thread instead of cotton, if available. If the material needs additional strength to hold the hem, simply add a ½-inch-wide strip of cloth. Fold over a protective layer of duct tape along the seine's bottom edge. Roll or fold the seine up and stow it in a pocket. To use, insert a couple of straight sticks into the hemmed side tubes, wade into the flow, plant the bottom of the seine firmly into the creek bed, and have a buddy kick around on the creek bottom a few feet upstream. Sixty seconds should give you enough bait for at least an hour or two of fishing. (Check local laws; some states prohibit catching live bait in certain waters.)

PLANT BOARDS IN YOUR YARD Coverboards are simply pieces of untreated plywood—chemicals in treated woods can leach into the ground below—placed on the ground in a shady spot and ignored for a few weeks. Once it's worked its magic, give it a lift to uncover earthworms, crickets, and beetle grubs—the Holy Trinity of live bait for panfish. A dinner-plate-size coverboard in a shady corner of your backyard should shelter enough crickets and worms for a quick after-work trip to the local pond. A full 4x8-foot plywood sheet might be home to a half-day's worth of serious bait dunking. Use a short stick with a protruding branch to lift up the edge of the coverboard—snakes like coverboards too—and remember to lower the coverboard gently back down to the ground to prevent damage to the creatures you've attracted.

GET THE LEECHES Ribbon leeches are irresistible to fish and a snap to catch. To load up, punch or drill a bunch of ⅜-inch holes in the sides of a coffee can, then bait it with hunks of bloody beef or fish heads. Smash the can shut with your boot, tie a length of box twine to the can, and place it in a few feet of water. Be sure to check the trap at sunrise. Leeches are nocturnal, and they'll check out of your coffee-can diner not long after daylight.

BASS

America's Fish. The crowd favorite. The funnel cake of fishing. The most sought-after gamefish in the land. Virtually everywhere and usually up for a good time. When most folks hear "bass" they think of the flagship of the fleet: the largemouth. That's the fish that's launched a million decal-splattered bass boats but is just as likely to be hauled out of granddaddy's farm pond. Then there's old bucketmouth's cool-water cousin, the smallmouth. He'll call a lake home as long as it's deep enough, but seems to favor rocky rivers.

Smallies, a.k.a. bronzebacks, are known for their hook-straightening power. Same goes for their distant kin, the striped bass. These brutes, which can top 50 pounds, live in the ocean and surge up freshwater rivers to spawn. They've also been successfully stocked in many landlocked reservoirs. Together, largemouths, smallmouths, and striped bass have been the source of more fun—and the cause of more skipped school days and unmown lawns—than anything else with fins. —T.E.N.

123 TAKE A HERO SHOT

Want to make a 3-pounder look like a 5-pounder? Use a wide-angle lens (there are a number of aftermarket ones for your smartphone), and have your buddy hold the fish well away from his body. Get close, low, and focus on the bass's eye. Gently shake the fish and it'll raise its fins and look even more impressive. Snap the pic and hit "post."

124 HELP YOUR KID BUILD A BASS PLUG

Most of us have more invested in fishing tackle than in our retirement plans, ignoring the fact that a bigmouth bass is just as likely to eat a lure made from a broomstick as it is a $12 articulated swimbait with a holographic paint job. Thankfully, the average 12-year-old has what it takes to make a DIY lure that'll catch the biggest bass in the pond. Here's how to lend a hand and stay out of the way at the same time.

Start with a 1-inch dowel cut to 3 inches in length. Use a rotary tool and sandpaper to shape the plug, but don't worry about replicating the shape of some famous manufactured lure. Go fat, go skinny, shape it like a snowman—just let the kid have some fun with it. Cup the mouth by drilling into the front of the plug with a drill bit just smaller than the diameter of the dowel. Raid the junk drawer for bling. Create a cool scale pattern by using the plastic net from a bag of vegetables as a paint stencil. Sprinkle glitter on drying paint or use glitter glue, and add other details with paint markers. Use thumbtacks for eyes, and paint eyeballs with a permanent marker. Add screw eyes, treble hooks, and a line ring at the popper face.

125 CRANK A RUBBER CRAYFISH

A bronzeback bass loves a crayfish above all other stream goodies, and nothing imitates a craw like a tube jig. It's not hard to fish a tube jig correctly, but it's very easy to do it wrong. Here's how to act like a bottom-dwelling creek crustacean.

DIAL IN DEPTH It's a delicate balance between enough weight to get the tube on the bottom, but not so much that it can't dance and swim. Rule of thumb: Use a ⅛-ounce jighead for still water less than 10 feet deep; a ½-ounce jighead for water 10 to 20 feet deep; and a jighead weighing ⅜ ounce for water deeper than 20 feet. Ratchet up the weight for moving water.

CONTROL SCENT Jam a small piece of scent-soaked sponge into the tube.

CRAWL ALONG Let the jig hit bottom by falling on a slack line. Reel up the slack and count to 10. Often, a bass will suck it in during the first few seconds. Now, start a series of rod-tip lifts—raise the tip, drop it, reel in the slack. The jig should swim a foot off the bottom, then flutter back down.

GO IN DRAG If swimming the jig fails, slow to a drag. Lift the rod tip very slowly, dragging the jig along the bottom at intervals of 6 inches to a foot. Set the hook at any hesitation.

126 STEER A SHINER TO A BIG HAWG

If you want a pig in the boat, nothing works better than a live shiner. A mouthful of minnow will fool the most lock-jawed largemouth, but first you have to get the bait to the bass. One neat trick is to fine-tune where you thread the hook through the bait to help steer shiners into different kinds of structure. A shiner hooked through the lips tends to swim back to the boat or stay in one place. A hook through the base of the dorsal fin creates plenty of bait action as the minnow tries to swim away and will often splash on the surface. To get the bait under floating mats of vegetation, hook it just above the anal fin. The shiner will swim away from the boat, and by gently lifting and dropping the rod tip a few times, you can get the bait to swim deeper and deeper.

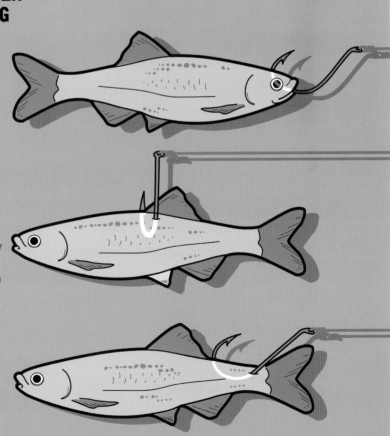

127 TAKE A DATE FISHING

Many a redneck has taken a first date fishing, knowing that there are worse places for a blossoming romance than a bass pond. If you're taking a lady fishing who's never been before, keep these rules in mind.

RULE 1 Avoid shad guts, rooster livers, and stinkbait. In fact, avoid catfishing altogether.

RULE 2 A farm pond full of aggressive 12-inch bass and a Pop-R is better than a chick flick and flowers.

RULE 3 For now, backlashes and crankbaits hung in your ear are cute. If this goes well, there'll be time for yelling down the road.

RULE 4 Be sure the boat's running perfectly ahead of time. A cussing meltdown while adrift with a dead motor is awkward for everyone.

RULE 5 *"Jesus, what a snake!"* Don't say that.

128 FISH A GOLF COURSE

Of course there are lunker bass in the lake next to the No. 9 green—why else would they hang those "No Fishing" signs there? Few golf courses open fishing to the masses, but getting permission to throw a few casts in the water hazards is often just a matter of asking the course superintendent. Go fishing early in the morning, before the course opens and while the greens are being mowed, then get the hell out of there before the golfers show up, so you aren't confused for one.

129 ID A GREAT BASS POND

Long before I ever stepped into a real bass boat or looked at a depthfinder screen, I learned to catch bass by bank- and wade-fishing small ponds, pits, and sloughs. Though a 2-pounder was big in most of them, a special few coughed up bucket-headed bass rivaling anything I've ever caught in a big-name lake. The spots where I caught those big fish all had some things in common.

FERTILE WATERS Some of the strip-mine lakes I fished as a kid were gin clear, but the best ones had a little stain. Slightly stained water means better fertility. Better fertility means more food for little fish, which in turn means more food for big fish. It's the circle of life. Stained water helps hide the heavier line you need to fight big bass, too.

GOOD COVER Baitfish need cover to hide in and survive from predators, but big largemouths also spend most of their days resting in cover. The more laydowns and weedbeds there are in a given pond, the more places a big bass can hide.

A SHADY SIDE Man-made ponds are typically shallow at one end and deep alongside the dam. Many times, landowners allow the dams of those ponds to grow up, especially with overhanging willows. Those deep, shaded sides (6 to 20 feet deep, depending on the pond) provide both respite from the summer heat and supplemental cover when lay–downs are not available. —W.B.

130

WIN THE LOCAL DERBY

Long ago, two rednecks met up on the bank of a southern lake, each hauling a stringer of largemouth bass. One of them said, "Shoot, my string's heavier'n yours."

The other redneck replied, "Pfft. Fifty dollars says it ain't."

And thus, the great American sport of tournament bass fishing was born. Of course, you don't have to wear a sponsor-laden jersey and drive a $70K glitter boat to enjoy some friendly bassin' competition. Local jackpot tournaments are held on lakes throughout the country. Fishing them is a ball, and they rarely cost much to enter. But win one, and you'll be flush with enough cash for a new shotgun. Since you'll be competing against a field of expert local anglers on their home waters, don't expect an easy trophy. But you can up your odds with this advice from a couple bass pros.

SCOUT IT OUT "Pay particular attention to the community fishing areas," says Terry Bolton, a full-time touring pro from Kentucky. "Local anglers tend to flock to them during tournaments. You don't necessarily want to avoid them because, hey, they're proven spots. But if you want to win, you better have some backup places in mind."

USE THE RIGHT LURE "Smallmouths are more aggressive and school up more often than largemouths," says Joe Balog, a smallmouth pro who dominated tournaments for years on lakes Erie and St. Clair. "When you're prepping for a smallmouth tournament, choose a lure that casts far and runs well at speed to cover water and find the biggest schools out there. I like a Rapala DT10. Keep looking until you find the biggest school of the biggest bass within the time limits of the tournament."

131 TWITCH CYPRESS KNEES

Paul Keith is a bass-fishing guide who grew up on cypress-laden Caddo Lake, which straddles the border of Texas and Louisiana. Like many southern lakes, cypress knees are full of big bass once the water reaches 50 degrees in early spring. Here's how Keith catches them.

TICKLE THE KNEES "I'm usually casting a weightless soft plastic at the trees," he says. "I'm always looking for the dark side of the trees. If the sun's bright, I throw to the shady side. I don't work the lure all the way back to the boat. If I don't get bit pretty fast, I reel up and cast to the tree from a different angle. A buddy of mine set the lake record a few years ago, fishing like this. That bass was a 16½-pounder."

KEEP IT SIMPLE "I'm not the kind of guy who uses five different rod types and actions for five different baits. A 6½-foot medium-heavy rod and a reel with a 6.3:1 retrieve ratio works fine for about everything I do. Spool up with 15-pound mono and you're good to go."

KEEP IT SLOW "I like something with a slow fall, usually a Zoom Fluke or Senko-style plastic," Keith says. "My personal favorite is the 5-inch V&M chopstick rigged on a 4/0 Bass Pro XPS O'Shaughnessy hook."

132 NIGHT FISH FOR LARGEMOUTHS

Mitch Looper is a big-bass fanatic from Arkansas. His largest fish to date weighed 14.41 pounds—one of the biggest northern-strain largemouths ever recorded. Most of Looper's trophy catches come from small lakes, and his favorite time to catch them is at night in late February.

FIND THE SPOT "I focus my attention on shallow, flatland lakes that time of year because they warm the fastest," Looper says. "I'm looking out for weedbeds, especially isolated ones. There may be a continuous stretch of weeds 100 yards long, but I want to fish the one section of weeds isolated from the rest. It may be the size of a kitchen table. Ideally, there's a deeper channel that swings in close to it."

TIME IT RIGHT "I fish as much as I can around the full and new moons, and I like to fish my best spots in the hour before and after the moon is either rising or setting," says Looper. "I prefer cloudy nights with some wind to break up the surface a little. I'm hitting that weedbed from every angle, and if it's in the middle of the bay, I may come back and hit it several times during a trip. When a big female is feeding, she's on the move. She's not just sitting there. You might intercept her at any time."

TOTE A BIG STICK "I like a heavy-action 6½-foot rod and a reel with a 7:1 retrieve rate," he says. "Big bass swim more quickly than small ones, and that fast reel makes a huge difference when fighting them. I use heavy line—25-pound mono or heavier—whenever I can get away with it."

CHUNK A JIG "I'm a jig freak. I particularly love swimming them if it's warmer and the fish are aggressive, but early on, when it's cold and sluggish, I'll fish them slow," Looper says. "To me, a jig should either take 30 seconds to retrieve . . . or five minutes."

133 CATCH A POND LUNKER

Pond bass will grab a crankbait or smash a topwater, but I've caught more 5-plus-pounders on two specific presentations than everything else combined. The average pond doesn't see a big number of boats every day like your favorite lake, but a single angler can educate a bunch of bass in a short amount of time. Chances are, the biggest bass in a given pond have been hooked at some point in their lives. If a lure doesn't look real, then they aren't biting it.

Sight-casting to shallow cover is the name of the pond-fishing game, and for that it's tough to beat a Zoom Super Fluke rigged Texas-style and weightless on a wide-gap worm hook. It can be walked across the surface or just under it when you need to cover water, or slowly retrieved through a stump bed, one twitch-and-fall at a time. Its big profile attracts larger bass, and it's heavy enough to throw with a baitcaster. I like a medium-heavy 6½-foot rod and 12- or 14-pound monofilament.

Some of the biggest pond bass will ignore a Fluke or any other artificial lure, but they won't pass up a live bluegill. Bluegills and other sunnies are a key part of the forage base in any good bass pond, and they're easy to get. They aren't legal bait everywhere, so check your regs.

Tackle is simple: Carry an ultralight rig to catch and keep handy two or three lively 4- to 5-inch bluegills. You

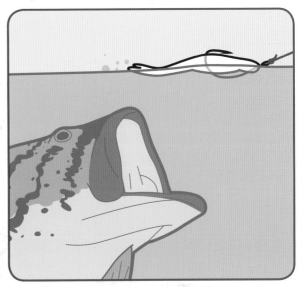

also need a flipping stick with 30-pound braid, with a 5/0 offset worm hook on the end. Hook the bluegill under the dorsal fin, about an inch forward from the tail, and clip a large cork—one just big enough that the bluegill can't pull it underwater—to the line 2 feet above the hook.

Cast to a laydown, weedbed edge, stump thicket, or other big-bass hangout, and wait. The bluegills initially try to swim for the heavy cover. The cork will slow him down, and that struggling will get the attention of a big bass if it's in the area. There's no mistaking the bite. —W.B.

134 'NECK UP A PORK RIND

One of the universal attributes of rednecks everywhere is a deep and abiding love of a good barbecue sammich. No surprise, then, that slapping a little pig on a bass bait can transform a slow day on the water to an epic one. An old-school pork rind helps imitate a crayfish when used with a jig—the venerable pig-n-jig—and mimics a frog when fished with topwater lures and spinnerbaits. But there's no reason to use pork rinds straight out of the jar, just like nobody drives a factory F-150 these days. Here are three ways to 'neck up a pork rind.

ACCESSORIZE Thread a strip of colored yarn through the rind's hook slit so it trails an inch behind

the end of the rind. Think of it like putting flame decals down your truck body.

SET A SCENE Slip the pork rind up your line about a foot above a lure, so your rig looks like a fish chasing bait. Don't use the premade hook slit, though—it's too large and the rind will slide down to the lure. Just punch a smaller hole through the pork rind with a sharp hook.

SHOW SOME SKIN Use a sharp knife to trim the fat off the last half inch of the pork rind, leaving the skin to flutter wildly.

SNAKES AND SMALLMOUTHS

The woman was standing in the Ozark gravel road in a bikini and flip-flops, grasping a dead timber rattlesnake by the neck. It was obvious that either she—or one of the two dirt-faced kids hovering at her hips—had smashed the pit viper's head real good with a rock. Its tail curled slightly in the way a fresh-killed snake's will—enough life to move a bit but not enough to buzz any alarm or thrash out of control. Fresh snake blood oozed across her thumb.

"Saw him layin' there in the road!" she beamed. It was a dandy, 5 feet long easy, and as thick as a man's arm. I doubt she'd have accepted a hundred dollars for it had you offered it up that very moment. "You'uns going down to the river?"

We weren't a half mile from the banks of the Jacks Fork.

"Yes, ma'am," Seymore said, putting his Blazer in park. I was in the front seat next to him. Robert and Rusty were in the back. We were going bass fishing, and Seymore told the woman so.

"Bass fishing? No bass in that river. But I hope you have fun," she said. Seymore put the Blazer into drive and continued on down the road.

"Brantley," Robert said as the water came into view, "That local woman says there's no bass in this river."

"She needs to stick to snakes," I said. "The bass are in here."

Dad had been taking my little brother and me to the Jacks Fork since we were kids, regaling us with stories of hard-fighting smallmouth bass.

I caught my first one when I was somewhere around 10, casting a crankbait to an eddy below a logjam, just downstream of where we were about to step into the water. It was well shy of the legal 18-inch mark, though, so I had to let it go.

We split up, two of us wading downstream and two upstream. We had little clear-plastic tackle boxes stuffed into our swimming trunk pockets, each fully stocked. It only took a few hours to convince everyone that there were, indeed, bass in the Jacks Fork River. Every eddy, undercut bank, and slow pool produced vicious strikes. We must've caught 50 smallies in a few hours. A couple of them even pushed 2 pounds.

"We ought to make this a tradition," Seymore said that night as we sat in the breezeway of the motel. "I mean, getting us all back together for a few days each summer wouldn't be hard."

"Think she ate that damn snake?" Robert wondered aloud. He was a master at keeping the subject light. We all quickly agreed that she'd skinned it and saved the rattles, and after some debate we were mostly satisfied that she'd fried it up and fed it to her kids too.

We went to bed late and woke up before daylight, so we wouldn't miss the early bite. We were there to go bass fishing, after all, and for that the Jacks Fork River rarely disappoints. —W.B.

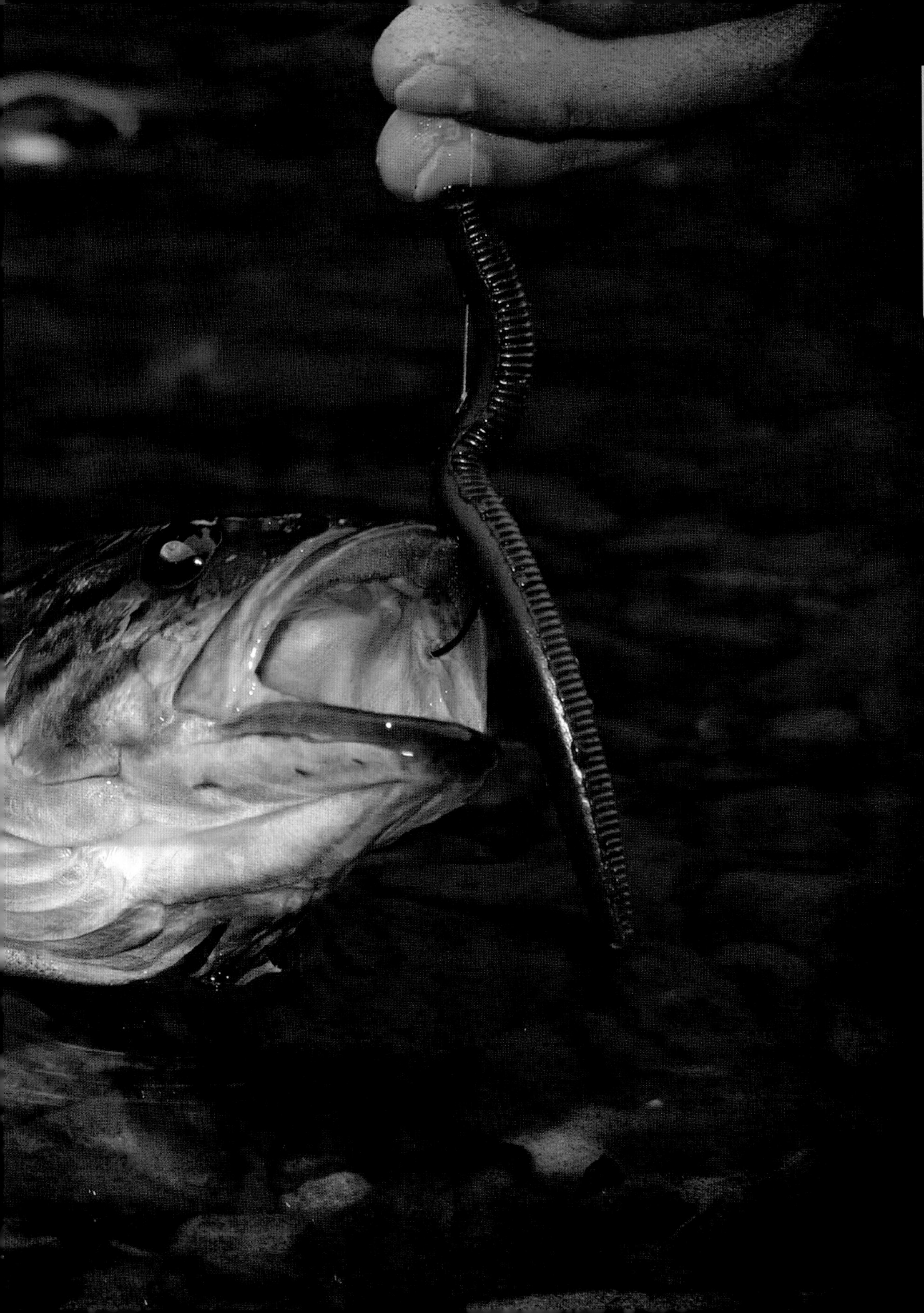

135 WIN A SLIME FIGHT WITH AN EEL

The good news: Hog striped bass can't say no to an eel. The bad news: Rigging snot snakes has to be the nastiest task in all of fishing. A medium-size eel will wriggle and wrap its slime-covered self into a ball around your hook, your hand, and any other body part in the vicinity, so it helps to slow the eel down a bit before attempting to rig it to a hook.

CHILL IT OUT Carry eels in a cooler with ice or a plastic reusable ice pack. Once they hit the water, they'll snap back to slimy life.

GET A GRIP If you've never handled an eel, you can't imagine the slime you have to deal with when grasping it firmly behind the head. Squares of burlap can help tame the slime, and I know of one angler who grabs eels with a Scotch-Brite pad folded in half. Even so, he says, he has to wash out the pad every so often because it gets so gunked up.

GIVE IT A WHACK Many anglers will whack an eel on the boat's gunwale to stun it, but take it easy so you quiet it down, not just knock it senseless.

BAG IT Another slime lizard handling method is to place it inside a zippered plastic baggie, hooking it through the baggie, and using scissors to cut away the plastic before you cast.

136 HOOK A LANDLOCKED ROCKFISH

Throughout the South, striped bass have been stocked in major lakes. Fishing for these brutes is popular throughout the spring and summer. Many local anglers hook them by fishing live herring (a.k.a. skipjack) on three-way bottom-bouncing rigs. Here's how.

COLLECT THE BAIT Late in the summer, young herring are 4 to 6 inches in size—big enough to bite the tiny jigs on a sabiki rig. With a heavy sinker on the end for casting

distance, toss the rig into the boils and work it quickly back to the boat. If there are young skipjacks in the area, they'll latch on fast. An aerated baitwell keeps them alive.

RIG FOR BASS Use a 6½-foot baitcasting rig, and tie a three-way swivel on 20-pound-test monofilament. To one eye of the swivel, tie a 6- to 10-inch dropper line, tipped with a pencil weight of 2 to 3 ounces (you may need to go heavier, depending on the current). On the other eye, tie a 2-foot, 14-pound-test leader with a 2/0 Kahle-style hook.

GET FISHING Run your boat right up into the discharge boils below the dam. Get squared away, pointing the bow upstream for a straight drift. Hook a lively herring through the eyes. Drop the rig over the side and let the current push the boat along, using your trolling motor to stay straight. Continuously bounce the rig on the bottom, keeping it as vertical as possible. Tailraces are full of snags, and if the boat gets ahead of the line, you can expect to get hung up.

HOOK 'EM Big rockfish will inhale a wounded herring that drifts by them. When you feel a strike, take up slack, feel for the fish, and set the hook. It's not unheard of to catch a big blue catfish doing this, either—and folks like us don't mind that one bit.

137 SURF-CAST LIKE A CANNON

The world-record distance cast is a mind-blowing 839.25 feet, nearly the distance of three football fields. Pin down a good off-the-beach cast, and striped bass cruising beyond the breakers will learn to fear your pickup truck. You'll need a shock leader of about three times the test of your fishing line and plenty of beach to practice.

STEP 1 Face the water, left foot forward. Twist your upper body 90 degrees to the right, and look away from the water. Drift your rod tip back and let the sinker or lure drop to the ground at the 3 o'clock position. Move the rod to about the 1 o'clock position. Drop the rod tip until your left arm is higher that your right. Reel in the slack.

STEP 2 Keep your right arm straight. With the sinker or lure on the beach, rotate your body at the hips, rod still behind you but moving in a smooth, circular pattern trending upward. Rotational energy fires the cast.

STEP 3 As your body straightens, shift your weight to the left foot, pull your left arm sharply down and in, and push with your right arm. Practice the timing of the release to straighten out any curve in the cast.

138 FISH A BASS ORGY

During a spawn, as many as 20 male striped bass will swarm a female; where stripers are called rockfish, this is known as a "rock fight." In many spawning rivers, the action is best at sunrise and sunset. Striped bass often spawn right in the rapids and riffles, so find a good spot to post up, and look for surfacing fish.

With a rock fight in view, fire a splashy surface plug like a Zara Spook across the water. Aim for the far side of the commotion, and crank the bait right through. Hold the rod tip high and "walk the dog" to get that zig-zagging side-to-side action from the plug: Snap the tip sharply, wait a half second to let the lure pop to the side, then keep pumping and snapping. Lower the rod tip as the lure nears the boat . . . unless you're in the mood for ducking trebles.

If you know you're in a good spot but not seeing any topwater action, chunk your plug into eddies and slow current breaks to create a commotion to draw male stripers cruising for a fight. Crank as many plugs as there are anglers on the boat. That's often all it takes to stir up another rock fight—the kind with a hooked striper on the line.

TROUT AND FLIES

Trout are out there, most everywhere you care to look—and they're hungry. Generally speaking, there are two kinds of trout fishing: Casting for wild, reproducing fish mainly in wild, untouched waters and targeting hatchery-raised stocked trout in nearly wild, nearly untouched waters, as well as in muddy ponds at RV campgrounds.

Happily, trout can be caught on just about any tackle, including conventional spincasting gear, big levelwinds for deep-water fish, fly rods, and cane poles. Depending on where you fish, you might catch a native cutthroat whose genetic makeup has not changed since the last glaciers left North America, a sterile, farm-reared fish grown fat on Purina Trout Chow, and everything in between. Brook trout, rainbow trout, and brown trout are the most common, but regional races abound, plus mutant strains like tiger trout.

Unfortunately, almost everyone who fishes for trout thinks their way is the only way and that everybody else is on the winding road to the Bad Place. Best thing to do is to figure out what works for you, and, while everyone else is arguing, go catch fish. —T.E.N.

139 EMBRACE POWERBAIT

Sooner or later you're going to tire of cheese dribbling through your treble hooks and sticky marshmallow fingers. You're going to get fed up with getting outfished by every Earl on the creek. Sooner or later you're going to try PowerBait, so you might as well know how to rig up for this finest of the redneck trout tactics.

PowerBait is a moldable, doughlike artificial bait that acts like a pizza bomb going off in the water. Love it or hate it, PowerBait levels the trout-fishing field and turns every so-so angler into a total warrior on hatchery water. High art it's not, but it's as close as there is to a sure thing on the river. And rigging it is as easy as falling off a rock.

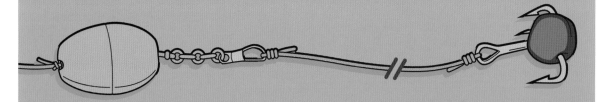

STEP 1 Thread 2- to 6-pound monofilament line through a ⅛- to ½-ounce egg sinker.

STEP 2 Tie a size-12 or size-14 barrel swivel to the line, and an 18-inch leader to the other end of the barrel swivel.

STEP 3 Tie a size-16 or size-18 treble hook to the line, and bait it with a glob of PowerBait rolled into a ball. Cast. Reel. Eat.

140 SERVE FISH A CASSEROLE

Behold, the Holy Trinity of redneck side dishes and trout baits alike: corn, cheese, and itty-bitty marshmallows. Talking them up to anyone who puts on airs might get you chased out of your local Trout Unlimited chapter, but, by golly, this trio of grocery store staples will stack up the trout.

 **CORN** Fresh off-the-cob corn won't cut it nearly as well as whole kernels from the scratch-and-dent bins over near the pork scrapple. Maybe it's because hatchery trout chow contains corn, maybe it's because a corn kernel is about the size of a trout pellet, or maybe it's because corn looks like a trout egg. But newly stocked trout will whack corn above anything else. Juice your bait with a salt-and-garlic bath overnight.

 **CHEESE** Nothing works like store-bought Velveeta. It can wash off the hook, though, so keep the block in a cooler until you're ready to carve a hunk for bait. Push the eye of a treble hook through a ball of the cheese until it's on the shaft. It'll seat down on the hook with the force of your cast. If you want to get complex, melt Velveeta in a pan and add garlic, salt, cornmeal, and bread crumbs, and it'll hug the hook tighter.

 **MARSH-MALLOWS** Tiny ones like those you sprinkle into hot chocolate seem to turn stocked trout inside out. Like corn, it could be that they resemble trout pellets or fish eggs, but they'll load up a stringer in a hurry. One bonus for fishing marshmallows is that they float, and even trout that aren't above eating Velveeta, corn, and marshmallows don't want to dig a meal out of the muck.

141 SHOW THEM THE SIZZLE

Hatchery trout get a bum rap for being as dumb as a sack of hammers, but that's not really fair. It's more a matter of them being uneducated. Having grown up in a concrete swimming pool, with pellet grub delivered daily, they might not be drawn to the most carefully tied Yallerhammer dry fly. But something in that tiny trout brain recognizes the flash of a fin and the sight of a baitfish skedaddling across the stream.

That's why chunking in-line spinners might seem old school but can be the way to rule the river on opening day. Go for tried-and-true spinners like Yakima Rooster Tails, Mepps Aglias, and, for deeper water, Blue Fox Vibrax Bullets. In-line spinners are particularly deadly on small, brushy backcountry waters, where an angler with an ultralight outfit and a good throwing arm can outfish just about anything but a light load of dynamite. Or so daddy said.

142 FISH A SURE THING

You can bust your fanny to get to remote backcountry trout waters, or you can back your mud tires to the edge of the water and catch fish from the tailgate. Nothing is guaranteed in life, but if you can't catch trout at one of these places, you need to give away your Ugly Stiks.

STOCKED STREAMS Nearly every state publishes detailed schedules for trout stocking in public waters. You won't win style points by tailgating the stock truck, but there's something to be said for filling a stringer with trout with minimal effort. And many states have moved to managing some stocked trout streams as "delayed harvest waters." Keeping fish is limited to certain times, but fishing remains open for folks who just want to catch them for fun.

PAY PONDS The only thing you need to bring to a pay pond is your wallet and a cooler. Private ponds often provide tackle, bait, nets, and fish-cleaning services. You don't even need a fishing license. Only catch is, you keep everything you catch, and you pay by the pound. It ain't *A River Runs Through It*, but to fill a cooler or turn a kid on to fishing, pay ponds are a hoot.

143

DITCH YOUR TREBLES

It doesn't take a math genius to figure out why treble hooks are effective, but they have some big downsides too. Trebles are wicked on a trout's soft mouth, certainly increasing the mortality rate on released fish. They can take much longer to remove than a single hook and are far more likely to hang up on submerged vegetation, rocks, and woody structure.

The fix is cheap and easy: Swap out trebles with single Siwash hooks. They'll save you time, save the trout distress, and won't tear up fishing nets either. First, determine which size Siwash you need to replace each treble on your trout lures (you can find replacement hook charts online). Then, it's a simple matter of removing the trebles from the split rings and replacing them with the Siwashes.

Once you're rigged, test each lure to see how it behaves in the water. Inline spinners smaller than size 2 might not run true without a treble, and crankbaits and stickbaits built for slashing and thrashing back and forth could foul. But for lures that will run true without trebles, single Siwash hooks will both save fish and lower your blood pressure.

144 GO TINY WITH A CASTING BUBBLE

Casting light flies and tiny lures with a spincasting rig is impossible without a casting bubble. These hollow, clear-plastic, bobber-shaped things add enough weight to zing dry flies, popping bugs, and even mealworms a country mile. It seems like cheating, but it can't be, because they sell all this stuff at Bass Pro Shops.

Casting bubbles are made a few different ways. Some have removable rubber stoppers, so the line can pass completely through the device. Others require tying on a barrel swivel, to which you attach an 18- to 36-inch leader and your lure, fly, or bait. But they all work the same way: You pull out a stopper or plastic spike and fill the casting bubble with lake or stream water. What's cool is that you can fine-tune the bubble's weight and buoyancy depending on how much water you let inside.

145 CATCH A NIGHT MONSTER

The biggest fish in many a trout river is a pig brown trout that's as nocturnal as a late-December 10-pointer. Your best shot at pulling it out of an undercut creek bank cave might be a bass lure designed back in your granddaddy's day. A topwater Jitterbug pushes a ton of water, splashing and gurgling with a fat, juicy silhouette against the night sky. You can eat dinner with the family, tuck the kids in, and be on the water in plenty of time for prime-time brownies. You don't have to overthink it. You don't have to be superclose to structure or cover. A hangry brown trout—one that's so hungry it's angry—will travel up to 4 miles a night to feed. Just get to the water quietly, without a light, and give Pappy's old bass plug a new lease on life.

146 COOK TROUT ON A STICK

On the southern coast of Spain you can buy *espeto de sardinas* right on the beach. They're skewers of fresh sardines cooked on a wood fire, and the first time I saw them I thought: "Heck, I can cook a trout like that back home on Wilson Creek." No grill, no utensils, nothing but a jackknife and fingers. This surely is the greatest country on earth, we don't know *everything* over here on the left side of the Big Pond.

What makes this method so quick and easy is that you don't have to wait for hot coals. First, cut a green stick a couple feet long, with a 2-inch branch stub on the fat end and 6 inches of stick beyond the stub. Sharpen both ends of the stick. Clean a trout, and insert the skinny end of the stick through the mouth, then run it the length of the fish, as close to the spine as possible. If you're cooking small stocker trout, you can run the stick perpendicular to the fish and stack three or four on a single stick.

Now, push the fat end of the stick into the ground so the fish is angled slightly. Build a teepee fire next to the fish, and start roasting. Turn the fish over once before eating. —T.E.N.

147 FISH A BREAM BED

For sheer action, it's hard to do much better than casting flies to spring-spawning bluegills. In ponds and lakes, look for sloping, sandy flats near deep water that are Swiss-cheesed with beds. In rivers and streams, check out woody cover near hard bottoms and shallow water. A single dinner-plate-size crater can hint at dozens more nearby. And no matter where you live, look for excuses to skip work on the full moons of spring and early summer, when a spawning peaks and every cast can land a fish.

PRESPAWN Prior to breeding, 'gills suspend offshore from spawning flats, so find channels near hard sloping ground and mid-lake humps. Back off into 5 to 15 feet of water and cast a weighted fly trailing a black ant.

SPAWN As water temperatures nudge 65 degrees, females move up to the bream beds, followed by the bucks. Spawning peaks when the water hits about 75 degrees. You can't go wrong with sponge spiders, hairy nymphs, and even popping bugs. But the key is stealth. Stay as far from the beds as your casting ability allows, and fish the outer edges of the spawning beds first, then work your way in.

POSTSPAWN Breeders need time to recover and will move into deeper water adjacent to the beds. Target root tangles, treetops, lily pads, and deep channels where the bottom falls steeply. Slowly twitch visible nymphs, such as a gold-ribbed hare's ear.

148 HUNT FOR FLY-TYING MATERIALS

Many common critters provide prime fly-tying materials, as long as you know what to clip, pluck, or cut, as well as how to store and maintain the materials: Simply salt the patch of fur you wish to keep. Deer tails require boning out. To keep bird feathers, store them in a zippered plastic bag or screw-top jar. To keep matched feathers from curling or getting smashed, tape the quills together and you'll have a perfect pair for streamer tails.

ANIMAL	FLY MATERIAL	FLY PATTERN
ELK	Bull neck-mane hair	Dry fly tails
ELK	Bull body hair	Elk Hair Caddis and parachute wings
WHITETAIL DEER	White belly hairs	Hair bugs
RINGNECK PHEASANT	Rooster tails	Knotted grasshopper legs; pheasant-tail nymph tails
RINGNECK PHEASANT	Church pane feathers	Simulated jungle cock for streamers
GRAY SQUIRREL	Tail hairs	Dry fly tails and wings; crayfish legs
WOOD DUCK	Barred body feathers	Classic streamer patterns; dry emerger tails
RABBIT	Fur strips	Leech and Rabbit Candy patterns; guard hairs for white streamer throats
SHARPTAIL GROUSE	Body feathers	Patterned body on tarpon flies
GRAY FOX	Guard hairs	Wiry collars on saltwater streamers
MALLARD	Breast feathers	Cheeks of Lefty's Big-Eye Deceiver
RUFFED GROUSE	Neck feathers	Hackles for wet flies
WILD TURKEY	Secondary wing quills	Wings for caddis flies, hopper patterns, Atlantic salmon patterns
HUNGARIAN PARTRIDGE	Neck and body feathers	Soft hackles
CANADA GOOSE	Secondary wing quills	Quill-wing patterns

149 GEAR UP

To teach kids about flyfishing, you'll need to get them the right equipment to learn with.

ROD Choose a soft-action rod so your kid can feel the rod flex and load. A modern fast-taper rod is a poor choice, as is a super-short rod. Any rod that deviates much from normal lengths has the tendency to get squirrely and is often more difficult for anyone to cast, let alone a noob. For starters, select an 8-foot 4-weight.

REEL At this level, a lightweight single-action reel is more than enough.

LINE Consider over-lining the rod by one line weight for easier turnover. Avoid long front tapers.

FLY Barbless hooks. Always. Tie a small knot next to the fly with blaze-orange egg yarn to make it more visible.

150 TEACH A KID TO FLYFISH

If helping Junior with his math homework makes you want to pull your hair out, you might wonder if you'll ever have the patience to school him on flyfishing. But kids love the mechanics of flyfishing, as well as the fact that they actually get to do something even when the fish aren't jumping on the hook. The trick is to approach it just like dog training. You're not going to take a puppy out for three long hours of retrieving. Figure you have a half hour of quality instruction time before the young'un gets bored, and make the most of it.

151 PREP YOUR LESSON PLAN

Once you've got the gear in hand, it's time for a lesson plan.

SET GROUND RULES Tailor your comments to the child's age. A 14-year-old might understand "feeling the rod load," but not an 8-year-old. Bring two rods so you don't have to take the rod from a kid's hand, and, above all, don't let him get bored. Skip perfection, and introduce new stuff quickly.

TEACH STROKE SCHOOL Start off with sidearm casts so the child can watch the line and better understand casting. Seeing the fly line reacting to stopping and loading the rod and line arcs make it easier to get the idea.

HAVE PHONE FUN Tell the child to treat the rod like a phone: Bring the rod up, say, "Hello, who is this?" and then set the phone down. That's the basic movement: Sweep the rod back, stop it, let the rod load, then a forward cast.

TRY A ROLL CAST If the child catches on to the basics of picking line up and putting it down, great. If he struggles, move quickly to roll casting. It's easier to learn, and with a bit of success he'll be ready to tackle a standard cast.

152 TIE A FLY WITH TRUCK TRASH

Whoopsie daisy. Just lost your last fly in that willow over the pond dam? No sweat. If you have any small bait hook and a tube of superglue you can stay in business till sunset (assuming you can stay out of the willow).

FLY BODIES Look for flexible materials that can be wrapped around a hook. There are probably three pairs of broken headphones stuffed into the back-seat pocket. Strip out the colored wires and pay close mind to any copper, which can be used for deadly Copper John nymphs. Thin foam insulation can be cut into strips, folded, and glued or tied to a hook. Finish with short snips of rubber bands, and you might not ever pay hard cash for a bream popper again. Old tan rubber bands wrapped around a hook make knockout mealworm flies. Do the same with wire twist ties.

FLY WINDS Dig deep into that back-seat landfill. The fat drinking straw from a long-ago Big Gulp makes super wing material because it's pre-bent in the perfect shape. For lighter wings, strip off the outer layer of a piece of Tyvek. Or take a thin piece of plastic garbage bag, stretch it until it's nearly translucent, and snip out wings. It's a perfect, near-weightless material some fly-tiers use even on their showroom models.

TROUT FISHING WITH KENNY DEAN

On my first morning in Calico Rock, Arkansas, I awoke to the sight of Kenny Dean sitting on the toilet. The door to the bathroom worked just fine, but it was like the thought of a constitutional without an audience never occurred to Kenny. He was beaming from ear to ear and yelling at my dad, who was still asleep. "Jimmy! Jimmy, get up! We have to get this boy out there to go fishing," he said. "He's going to catch a big brown today, I just know it."

At 14 years, I didn't need any extra coaxing to get up and get dressed. The room smelled like wet waders, outboard gas, and whole-kernel corn from the previous evening's foray. I'd already caught my fill of the 'bows; what I wanted was a five-pound brown trout for the wall. I retied the crankbait—a Rapala CountDown Minnow—that I'd been casting the evening before. Kenny said it would work as well as anything to catch a big trout, and when it came to fishing, I trusted him over anyone else.

Kenny was a lawyer (a good one, Dad said) but he kept a boat hitched up to his car, even parked at the courthouse. I mainly thought of him as a professional fisherman of sorts, since we hadn't had that many interactions that didn't involve fishing. He grew up in Arkansas, so he was the perfect guide for a White River trip.

We hit the river that day with half a dozen spinning rods rigged with crankbaits and corn spinners, along with Dad's fly rod, which mostly remained on the floor of the boat. Kenny brought several cans of Beanee Weenee too, because he was prone to low blood sugar, and Beanee Weenee was the surest of all cures for that. It was 90 degrees by noon, when Dad tied up the boat in the shade of a river bend to eat lunch. The White's modest current kept the boat swaying gently against the tether. Kenny leaned back in his seat and sang. "Under the shade of the beech nut tree, little Will Brantley there sat. He was amusing himself by . . ."

"Kenny!" Dad interrupted. "Don't you teach him that song."

Kenny just smiled. Five minutes later, he whispered the remainder of the tune in my ear. It was the filthiest thing I'd ever heard.

Later that night, the room again smelled like wet waders and trout slime. Dad and Kenny were kicked back on the motel beds, sipping whiskey from the same stainless Thermos lids they'd used as coffee cups that morning and tobacco spitters at midday. Exhausted from the casting and the sun, I turned on the sink to brush my teeth, took in a mouthful of water, and immediately spat it out.

"Ugh! This water tastes awful!" I said. "Dad, I'm gonna have to rinse my mouth out with some of your whiskey."

Kenny belted out his signature rapid chuckle. "You hear what he said, Jimmy?"

"Yes," Dad said, fighting back his own smile. "I heard it."

It was a good detail shared at just the right time. And with it I'd earned my right to stand there and laugh with the men. —W.B.

FISH WITH TEETH

Some fish really bite back—which seems only fair, right? But we're not talking about those little clam-crushing teeth in the back of a shellcracker's throat. These are bloodletting, flesh-shredding fangs sharp and numerous enough to pulverize a good eating-size trout. There are plenty of predatory freshwater fish equipped with nasty chompers. Many of these meat-eaters grow so big you have to use lures that look like they came from a junkyard. Giant spinnerbaits with 10/0 blades that feel like garbage can lids as you rip them through the water. Heavy lead-core lines trolled a country mile behind the boat and at depths where the fish are practically blind. This is where fishing meets back-alley brawling. —T.E.N.

153 TWITCH UP CHAINED LIGHTNING

The smallest gamefish in the pike family, a chain pickerel can reach 3 feet in length and weigh as much as 7 pounds, though most are just a couple pounds of pure fury. These bantamweight predators pack all the bad attitude and needle-sharp teeth of their bigger cousins, the musky and the northern pike.

Also known as jack pike, grass pike, and "chained lightning," pickerel like to wait and mug unsuspecting minnows and crayfish. They usually live on the wrong side of the tracks, in reedy backwaters and swampy ponds and river sloughs, and luring a spring-hungry chained pickerel to slash at a surface plug will wipe away the winter blues in a jiffy. Dial up the fun with an ultralight spinning rod and reel spooled with 6-pound-test. Monofilament works fine, but consider a 12-pound-test leader. Load up with small stickbaits and twitchbaits you can cast toward weeds, logs, rip-rap, and anywhere else you'd expect a thug to lurk. Twitch the lure and pause in an erratic cadence, and hang on tight for a slashing jab of chained lightning.

154 RIP HEAVY METAL FOR MUSKIES

The thing to know about muskies is that they're ambush predators. When they see baitfish trying to flee, it triggers a serious kill-it-now response in them. Sort of like what happens at your family reunion when there's just one last beer in the cooler. Jim Saric, editor of *Musky Hunter* magazine, takes the fight to the fish when he's cranking big swimbaits and spinners. To trip a musky's trigger, says Saric, try to bump structure with your lure on the retrieve. Don't shy from weeds and rocks. Purposefully steer crankbaits and spinners into the debris. When your bait bumps a rock, a log, or submerged vegetation, lower the rod tip to create slack, causing the lure to hesitate like a baitfish trying to figure its way out. Then, rip the rod tip back so the lure explodes from the cover. This will often trigger a strike from a musky sulking in the structure.

155

CATCH A PINT-SIZE WATER WOLF

Giant 45-inch pike from northern Canadian waters get all the buzz, but not many rednecks ever have the chance to hop a floatplane to fish a wilderness lake full of loons. We all know of a good river dam, though, with a mud beach that's perfect for bank-fishing and launching trunk-bed johnboats. And in early spring and again in the fall, midwestern pike will move into dam tailwaters and backwaters to pack on the pounds during those post-spawn and pre-winter periods.

Trophy fish might be a long shot in these waters, but filling a cooler with a mess of 20-inch "hammer handles" sure isn't. Fish deep with jigs tipped with soft baits, or use crankbaits for mid-depth pike. Perhaps the best bet is a backwater cove or eddy, where water slows and marshy reeds grow. Honker pike will lay up in the vegetation to ambush baitfish, crayfish, duck babies, and your carefully placed hair bug.

156 MAKE A DAM JIG

Vertical jigging for saugers and walleyes in tailraces is a productive wintertime technique. But finicky saugers are notorious short-strikers. Stinger rigs help, but saugers still can snip the monofilament line tied to the extra treble hook. Tennessee guide Jim Duckworth has an ingenious rig that replaces the mono with a snap-swivel connection.

STEP 1 Saugers might hold in as much as 50 feet of fast water in winter. For the jig to remain vertical at that depth, it must be heavy. Most tailrace jigs are ¾ to 1¼ ounce. Color only matters in less than 30 feet of water (there's no sunlight penetration beyond that). A favorite combo is an orange jighead with a chartreuse grub.

STEP 2 Snip off and save a slice from the head segment of a curly-tail grub. Slide the grub onto the jig.

STEP 3 Thread a No. 5 treble hook onto the snap of a No. 10 snap swivel, then run the swivel end over the barb of the jig hook. Slide the saved segment over the barb and move it down the hook until it rests next to the swivel. This will keep the stinger from slipping free.

STEP 4 Finish by tipping the jig with a big, lively minnow or shad and burying the stinger hook in its side.

157 FISH A LEECH

Live leeches are an excellent walleye bait. Even if the fish aren't biting, you can use a bait bucket full of them to frighten your children into behaving themselves. "If you kids don't quit rocking this boat, I'm gonna let the leeches suck the ornery outta ya!"

Whether you mean it or not, it's an empty threat. Historically, some species of leeches were used in medicine to suck "bad blood" out of sick patients, but ribbon leeches, the freshwater variety typically sold in bait shops, feed on dead fish and small invertebrates—not human blood.

Leeches are at their best during the open-water season, since they tend to ball up on the hook and not move when the water is too cold. You can tip a jig with one, pull it on a bottom-bouncer rig, or fish it under a slip bobber in shallow cover. Keep leeches fresh with a well-aerated baitwell, and go for the biggest, liveliest one you can grab when it's time to rig up.

158 HEAD SOUTH FOR YOUR TROPHY

To the chagrin of Midwestern and Canuck walleye fishermen, many of history's biggest specimens weren't caught from the great northern waters but way on down South. Here's a look at three of the biggest.

25 POUNDS Legend has it that the wife of Mabry Harper insisted on having this toad of a walleye—caught at Old Hickory Lake, Tennessee—officially weighed, measured, and photographed before Mabry took to it with a fillet knife and ate it for supper. Although the Freshwater Fishing Hall of Fame disqualified the fish due to some murkiness surrounding its actual size, it's still recognized as the world record by the International Game Fish Association.

22 POUNDS, 11 OUNCES On an early spring night in 1982 at Greer's Ferry Lake, Arkansas, Al Nelson hooked into this monster walleye while trolling a crankbait in his aluminum boat.

18 POUNDS, 4 OUNCES Mark Wallace, a Texan, traveled to Arkansas to do some walleye fishing in March of 1983 and set the 4-pound-test line-class record when he landed this fish at North Little Red River.

159 HAND-LINE A BIG WALLEYE

Big walleyes make spawning runs into major river tributaries in early spring. Trouble is, the fast currents and high, muddy water that time of year can make catching fish a challenge with traditional rod-and-reel techniques. This is when old-school walleye-loving rednecks break out the hand-lining equipment.

A hand-lining "reel" is a spring-loaded spool filled with wire line and mounted to the gunwale of a boat. At the end of the line, you attach a heavy weight—a pound or more of lead—and just above that are swivel snaps for attaching monofilament leaders tipped with crankbaits. Leaders are typically 25-pound-test or heavier and at least 15 feet long. Large, shallow-running minnow-shaped crankbaits in gaudy colors like chartreuse and orange are most popular.

Simply drop the weight to the bottom and creep along in your boat with the bow aimed into the current. Most hand-liners like to watch their electronics and work drop-off edges, which big walleyes use like highways in the spring. You hold the wire in your hand, and gently bump the weight along bottom, keeping the whole rig as vertical as possible. Strikes are usually pretty vicious. When you hook a fish, ease it to the surface, letting the reel automatically take in the wire slack until you can scoop the fish with your net.

HELL, I CAN CLEAN THAT!

NORTHERN PIKE

One of the best fish dinners I ever had was northern pike cooked in butter and garlic in aluminum foil over a campfire in the Minnesota Boundary Waters. My buddy and I sipped McMaster's Whisky, which seemed to enhance the pike's flavor as the evening wore on. Pike are the stars of many a shore lunch because they're easy to catch and provide plenty of meat. Some anglers curse them for their bones, but we didn't have any problems. Here's how we did it.

FILLET IT FIRST Various pike-cleaning methods require cutting around the infamous "Y-bones" and removing the meat in chunks. Since fish in your belly is the end result, these methods will get the job done, but we started by slicing behind the pike's gill plate and filleting each side, skin on, same as you would most any fish.

SKIN IT OUT Next, we used the edge of a sharp

fillet knife to separate the meat from the skin—again, same as with any other fish—and then to carve out the rib cage.

MAKE THE CUTS The Y-bones run the length of the fillet, right down the center. Removing them is similar to removing the mud line on a big catfish fillet. Using the tip of your knife, with the edge at an upward angle, cut below the Y-bone line, from one end of the fillet to the other. You'll be able feel the bones as you work. Next, turn the fillet around and make the same cut above the Y-bone line.

GET THE BONES Last, just grab the strip of meat containing the Y-bones at the front end of the fillet and peel it—and the bones—right out. It'll look something like a zipper, and it'll leave you with a luscious and boneless pike fillet ready to be enjoyed with cheap Canadian whisky. —W.B.

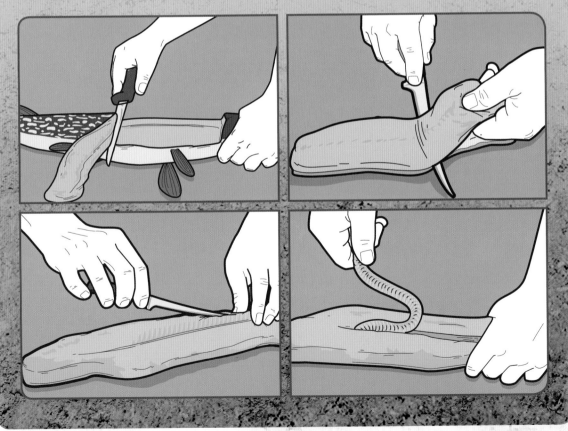

LEARN TO LOVE TRASH

Natural resources departments and fisheries biologists refer to these species as "rough fish." It's the politically correct term for freshwater fish that aren't gamefish (bass, walleyes, trout, and the like), and therefore aren't usually subject to things such as seasons, regulations, and limits.

Rednecks call them trash fish—but don't mistake that moniker for a term of derision. Truth is, when it comes to catching and eating species like drum, gar, carp, buffalo, and bowfin, rednecks are specialists. We know fun and food when it's swimming there in front of us, and that's why we'll hit the water armed with everything from rods to gigs to bows in search of our beloved trash. —T.E.N.

160 BUILD A BOWFISHING RIG

Really, the only way to make fishing better is to combine it with hunting and weaponry, and that's exactly what you get with bowfishing. Done day or night in the spring and summer, bowfishing requires minimal equipment and can produce quick success on big gar, carp, and other trash fish. Here's how to build your own bowfishing rig.

GET A BOW Most dedicated bowfishing bows have relatively light draw weights of 40 to 50 pounds, long axle-to-axle lengths, and little or no let-off, allowing for instinctive snap-shooting with fingers. A capture rest, such as a Cajun Fishing Biscuit or a Whisker Biscuit soaked in superglue (bowfishing arrows don't have vanes), helps keep the arrow in place. You can also use a recurve bow and shoot straight off the shelf.

ADD A REEL You can buy a fancy bowfishing reel, which will be worth every penny if you end up doing this a lot. If you don't want to sink a bunch of cash into a rig right out of the gate, you can also make your own "reel" by bolting a sports-drink bottle or small coffee can into the stabilizer port of your bow and wrapping the braided bowfishing line around that. When you shoot a fish, you simply pull the line in by hand and wind it back around the bottle.

RIG THE ARROW Most bowfishing arrows are made from fiberglass (though carbon models are available). They're extremely heavy and durable, and they'll last for years provided you don't lose them. The basics of a fish arrow include the point, the safety slide (where you tie in the line—typically pre-rigged), and the nock.

161 BEAT THE DRUM

On the saltwater flats, red drum—or redfish—are a game fish revered for their aggressive, hard-fighting personality and delicious fillets. In inland rivers and lakes, the freshwater drum (usually called simply "drum" or "sheepshead") has the same personality as a redfish, if not its culinary qualities.

When you hook into one, it's customary to say, "Aw hell, it's a drum," while secretly enjoying the fight. Like their saltwater cousins, freshwater drum will take a live-bait presentation off bottom, suck in a soft-plastic worm, slam a crankbait, and in the right scenario, put forth a noble effort at smacking a topwater lure. They don't jump when hooked, but they do make powerful, driving runs—and since they routinely top 20 pounds, those runs put a hurt on light tackle. No matter the water or weather conditions, get a lure in front of a drum, and it'll probably bite—and reeling in a fish is always better than going home skunked.

162 FIND THE BEST CARP

When it comes to eating the king of trash fish, some carp out there are better than others.

COMMON CARP I have eaten these invasive goldfish look-alikes. Overseas, they're captive-bred and an important food fish. Here in the states, the wild ones have an orange, muddy flesh laden with bones—as tasty as it sounds.

SILVER CARP Though also full of bones, the flesh of silver carp (they're the jumping ones) is white and flaky and tastes just fine. There is an effort to create a market for these highly invasive fish in hopes of sustaining a commercial fishery and hopefully controlling their numbers, but non-redneck America's acceptance of carp as cuisine is lukewarm at best.

BUFFALO FISH These native, carplike fish are very common as bowfishing targets on major lakes and rivers, and shooting them is an absolute blast when in spring they move into the backwaters to spawn. Fried buffalo ribs are a southern delicacy. Picture a rib bone wrapped in fried fish, rather than smoked pork, and you've got the idea.

163 TRY GAR BALLS

Gar flourished near the top of the aquatic food chain for millions of years before Cajuns discovered them. They're tough to catch with a hook and line, but a 12-inch piece of frayed nylon rope attached to a barrel swivel will entice topwater strikes and tangle in their teeth securely enough for you to land them.

You'll need tin snips to open a gar's hide, but they have backstraps that are shrimplike in texture. Chop the meat into small cubes and mix it with mashed potatoes, chopped onions, eggs, parsley, and Cajun seasoning. Roll the mixture into hush-puppy-size balls and—you guessed it—fry them in hot oil. It's not entirely different from a crab cake, especially after three or four beers. (Note: Gar eggs look like caviar, but if you eat them, they'll make you mess the bed, puke till your guts are empty, and wish for death. They're highly toxic to humans, so throw them away.)

164 TRICK OUT A BOAT

You can catch, shoot, spear, or even wrestle fish from shore—but sooner or later, every redneck really should experience the joy (and crippling debt and hassle) of boat ownership. No single boat will be suitable for all types of freshwater recreation, but the right one will let you catch bream, shoot carp, watch fireworks, pull a tube, and haul duck decoys.

GO ALUMINUM A big, glittering bass boat is certainly sleek and comfy—but you don't want to bounce it off a stump on a mud flat. Aluminum is the way to go for rednecks. It has about the best strength-to-weight ratio of any boat-building material out there, and it's virtually impervious to the elements. Bust a hole in the hull? Weld it back together. And, of course, you can get it with a slick custom camouflage paint job. Most all-purpose johnboats are 15 to 18 feet long and at least 48 inches wide across the beam. They're typically either modified-V hulls or true flat-bottom boats.

GET A SHOOTING DECK This platform on the bow of the boat allows a bowfisher or sight-caster to get a better view of fishy targets. It's also a good place for ladies in bikinis to gyrate or for you to demonstrate your "pee for distance" prowess (though not at the same time).

TROLL EASY You need an electric motor for silently creeping around the shallows and for getting back to the bank when you realize that you've packed more beer than gasoline. You can spring for a new Minn Kota or, like most rednecks, keep three well-used and semifunctional trolling motors in the garage at all times.

RUN FAST Many a redneck kid has learned all the colors of the rainbow by studying the two-stroke outboard oil slick left behind on the surface of the lake. New outboard motors, particularly four-strokes, are much easier on the environment, and they're so quiet that you can argue with your buddy about the merits of various stinkbaits without so much as raising your voice.

165 WRASSLE A MUDFISH

In polite company it's known as a bowfin. Out on the docks, this primitive beast is known as a blackfish, mudfish, dogfish, grinnel, cypress trout, or choupique. Even more commonly, it's referred to as a *"What the #*$! was that thing that just tore the #@$@*#! out of my bass plug?!?!"*

Bowfins lurk in the soupiest, shallowest, weediest, gunk-filled backwaters of eastern North America. They'll also venture into largemouth bass habitat to bust up tackle and fool anglers into thinking they have the next world record on the line when it's really just an ornery 3-pound bowfin. Not a lot of folks target bowfins, so few are prepared to de-hook a pissed-off primordial beast with a head as hard as concrete and jaws lined with teeth.

The first rule: Do not stick your fingers in a bowfin's mouth, unless you want to be known as "Stubby" for the rest of your days. Bowfin will thrash and bite long after they've been hauled out of the water. First, fight the green out of a hooked bowfin and haul it up only after it's wore out. Lip it with a gloved hand or a lip-gripping device. If you're onshore, drag the fish to a grassy bank and hold it down firmly as you twist out the hook. If you're in a boat and the bowfin weighs more than 6 pounds, there's nothing we can do for you. You are probably going to die.

166 CATCH GAR ON A ROPE

Catching these prehistoric beasts requires some funky gear. Gar have bony mouths, so hooking them is no easy feat. What's better is to hurl an entanglement lure that wraps around their fine teeth and narrow jaws, allowing you to haul them up on conventional tackle. Just remember: The trick to snaring gar is to hold off on setting the lure. When the fish strikes, give a bit of slack so the gar can work its fine teeth into the rope, shaking its head to snare it even more firmly. Then, apply pressure to bring the prehistoric beast aboard.

Making a rope entanglement lure is a snap. Here are three ways to do it.

REALLY EASY Cut 6 inches of yellow braided nylon rope and melt one end with a lighter or match. Unbraid the strands from the other end for two-thirds the length of the rope. Attach it to a stout leader with a slipknot, and chuck it into gar water.

NOTHING TO IT Fold a 12-inch length of nylon rope in half and cinch a plastic cable tie an inch from the bend. Untwist the rope strands and straighten them out. To attach it to your line, use the bend at the cable tie as an oversize hook eye.

NOT SO BAD Snip a 4- to 5-inch piece of ⅜-inch nylon rope. Loosen the fibers by twisting and pushing the rope in and out, then thread it onto the shank of a large hook. Melt the nylon to fuse the rope to the hook shank, wrap with braided line, and cover with epoxy. Untwist the strands, straighten them, and you're done.

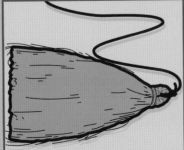
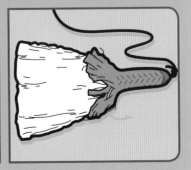

167 GIG A SUCKER

Maybe it's not really "fishing" per se, but sucker gigging still involves fish, boats, outboard motors, big lights, good friends, peanut oil, and beer—and all that's good enough for us. Sucker gigging is a beloved tradition in the Ozarks, a regional heritage born out of the cold and crystal-clear spring-fed streams that bubble up out of Ozark limestone.

Using johnboats—rigged with superbright lights and heavy custom-made gigs up to 16 feet long—locals will throng to the riverbanks on fall and winter nights. While giggers chase down golden redhorse suckers, northern hog suckers, and white suckers through the shallows,

shore parties break out over bonfires and deep-fat fryers crackling with fish and potatoes. There is music. There is beer and brown liquor—not to mention enough Carhartt overalls to carpet the planet.

Getting started in sucker gigging requires a bit of an investment. You'll need a johnboat large enough to float a generator, halogen lights, and gigs worthy of Poseidon. It might be best to take a hard look at your family tree and ask around. If you have any Missouri roots at all, start calling those third cousins twice removed. Sucker gigging is a family affair. Shouldn't be hard to score an invitation if you can prove you're blood kin.

WHAT THE #*&! IS A

SNAKEHEAD

The snakehead is the world's first "frankenfish." Originally developed in a laboratory, it's a fish that's half cottonmouth, half Godzilla. No, that's not right. But it's close. The snakehead is an invasive Chinese fish that first showed up here in 2002, having its babies in a Maryland pond. It's now spread across the Chesapeake Bay region and has been found in North Carolina, Florida, and other redneck strongholds. And it won't rest until it's eaten every last bass, panfish, native catfish, and shad in the country. The snakehead will even gulp air and then squirm across wet lawns at night to drag sleeping puppies out of children's bedrooms. No, that's not right, either. But it's close.

GUNS, GRUB & FUN

The boy was maybe eleven years old. We'd all been hunting hard since before sunrise because squirrel season had opened in the big woods around Ville Platte, Louisiana. Now, twelve hours later, I was hungry enough to eat a frozen dog, but my hosts were in no hurry. We skinned the gray and fox squirrels and put them in a stew of onions and peppers. When the cook slid the top on the Dutch oven, he said, "I'm puttin' 'em on 'drink,'" and that's exactly what we did for the next 3 hours. During that time, I managed to lose my shirt to an eleven-year-old in five-card draw.

In Evangeline Parish, the first Saturday in October has long been known as "Squirrel Day." Schools close early the day before Squirrel Day—some don't open at all—because attendance by students and teachers alike is halved. Businesses shutter their windows. Banks don't open. Everybody heads for "camp," which can mean a rough bivvy in the back of a pickup truck or a deluxe hunt lodge with electricity, air conditioning, and big-screen TVs.

When I pulled up to the McCauley family camp the day before the opener, a crowd was already on hand. Two guys were working on a fussy outboard motor while its guts simmered in a pot of water on a camp stove. An old man spoke encouragingly to his two great-grandsons as they dropped shiners through a trapdoor in the boat dock. More young boys on ATVs were raising clouds of dust on the dirt road. Stewed catfish simmered in a Dutch oven while three or four folks hovered over a homemade game they called "washerboard"—like cornhole, but with common washers instead of beanbags. Notably, it could be played one-handed, which was good since a beer was ever-present in the other.

We were hunting, but it seemed mostly an excuse to do a bunch of other fun stuff. A lot of it involved motors, knives, firearms, and cast-iron pots seasoned with three generations of black pepper and Crisco.

By my third morning out in Louisiana squirrel country, I was bleary-eyed and dragging, from hours of four-wheeling, hunting, card playing, beer drinking, and eating sausage and onions at midnight. For that morning's hunt, I was paired with a sixty-six-year-old man who was waiting on his four-wheeler when I stumbled out the camp door. He patted the seat behind him. I slipped an emergency kit into my coat pocket—a two-pack of Alka Seltzer and a fist-sized wad of toilet paper—and climbed on for the ride. —T.E.N.

PARENTING

Redneck kids aren't any different than other kids, except they know how to work a lockback knife, they know the best part of a fried bream is the tail fin, and they know it's okay to fart in front of Uncle Mark, but that they better hold it till their eyes bug out if Granny's around. They say strange and wonderful things like, "Yes, ma'am" and "No, sir, Daddy, I did not put oil in the chainsaw, and I'm really sorry, and it won't happen again."

Once, Julie and I were packing the truck with camping gear when our daughter Markie walked up. She could see we were headed somewhere for the weekend, and asked, "Mommy, will I pee-pee inside or outside?" Either was fine with her. Sometimes a girl just needs to know the deal.

I was pretty proud of that moment and another one, too. We were headed out the door to Sunday school one morning when Jack hollered down from the second floor. "Hey, daddy, can I take my hatchet to church?" Of course not, son. But thanks for asking.

That's just good home training. —T.E.N.

168 TEACH YOUR KID TO CATCH A SNAKE

They can learn this by trial and error, which can be fun to watch, but good parents put snake-catching on the parenting list of lessons somewhere between "learn exactly where the dog's chain snaps taut" and "use the house trailer jack to get the Bronco off Daddy."

First, make a positive identification to ensure that the snake is not venomous. This is a good time to teach a child how to carefully identify harmless snakes. A good lesson for starters is to avoid anything that looks like it could bite the snot out of you. Once you have determined that the snake lacks fangs and poison glands filled with enzymes that will make red blood cells swell and burst by the billions inside your leg, move in with confidence.

Pick up a stick or branch with your nondominant hand. You'll use this to wiggle and wave in front of the snake's head, so it won't focus on the fact that a large, sweaty, human hand is approaching it from behind.

Grab the snake between the base of the skull and the most superior cervical vertebra, a position known as "right behind the head." If it's a good grab—and you'll know instantly—then hang on tight no matter how much the snake whips and coils around your arm and poops a nasty foul-smelling, green-brown sludge from its anal vent that will take a week of scrubbing with shop soap to remove. This is okay: It's not really poop.

Now you have caught yourself a snake. Get a snapshot up on Facebook quick. Future employers will be more impressed by this than if you ever get your Eagle Scout patch.

169 SAVE YOUR LURES FROM YOUR LITTLE ONES

You'd have done the same thing. At the Bass 'N Boat Expo, my daughter Markie was fidgeting in the baby backpack and hampering my ability to fully concentrate on the subtle differences between the Glitter Pepper rubber worm color and the offering in Speckled Oil. But the booth was giving away 9-inch rubber spring lizards—no hook, of course—so I snatched one from the free sample bowl and handed it over my shoulder to li'l snookums. I didn't hear a peep from her after that.

It couldn't have been more than an hour or 4 later when I realized that the gargantuan salamander had vanished. Markie was at that precious stage where she ate rocks and bugs with the same gusto as Cheerios. You had to watch her like a hawk. So that explains the exchange with the triage nurse:

"She ate what?"

"Well, I'm not saying she ate it. I'm saying she might have. But let's say she did. Is that a bad thing?"

"She ate what?"

"Hold on, I'm just saying. What would 9 inches of quivering plastic formed in the shape of a very large salamander—down to the toes, you really should have seen this thing, it would crush a bedding bass—but what could that do to an 18-month-old child? It didn't have a hook in it."

"She ate what?"

So here's the lesson, and there's no reason for you to learn it the hard way. You just walk yourself and your precious bundle into the urgent care and lay it out straight and unvarnished: You have no idea where that child's mama was or what she was thinking, but it's a dang good thing you got home from the dirt track before that baby got to the crankbaits. —T.E.N.

170 TEACH A KID THE SEVEN FARTS

For his twelfth birthday, my younger brother, Matt, asked to go bluegill fishing with my dad and Kenny Dean. Kenny was a lawyer, originally from Arkansas, who mostly specialized in fishing, duck hunting, dirty jokes, and whiskey. When I was young, he nearly convinced me that he was my real daddy, and he was always singing these short little songs about some lady from Nantucket.

Matt's birthday weekend was a success. They camped, and he came home with grand tales of bluegills and little bass they'd fried over a fire and eaten with white beans. Plus, he said, Kenny had taught him all about the distinct types of farts, of which there are seven: fizz, fuzz, fuzzy-wuzz, poot, tally-poot, tear-ass, and rattler.

Our mother was thrilled with the lesson. Like a cherished recipe, it was passed on verbally through the generations, Matt and I have taught the seven farts to half a dozen or more youngsters worthy of such knowledge, usually while fishing or on opening morning of deer season. I know that my boy already gets a big kick out of flatulence, and so I expect him to have the full seven committed to memory by kindergarten. —W.B.

171 LEARN TO POOP IN THE WOODS

You'd think this procedure would be self-explanatory, but it's proof that in today's age, there are indeed still limits to unlimited data plans. When nature calls, your kid can writhe in misery, mess their pants, or take care of business in the woods and be back to rock-skipping in 10 minutes. The last option is the best, and the rules are relatively simple.

AIM DOWNHILL No exceptions.

DON'T WEAR HOODS They can catch things.

BRING TP If you forget, take a pocketknife to the corner of your T-shirt.

SHINE A LIGHT If it's dark, you don't want to have to peel a canebrake rattlesnake off a bare butt cheek.

FIND A FORKED LOG It's nature's toilet seat.

BURY THE BUSINESS Dig, do, and dispose. I don't know of anyone who actually does this (and even fewer who'd volunteer to enforce it), but it's evidently what the Scouts teach.

KEEP YOUR GUN HANDY At least if you're hunting, because game animals have the uncanny ability to appear when your rear is exposed.

172 GET A REDNECK KID TO EXERCISE

According to the Centers for Disease Control, children need at least 60 minutes of physical activity per day. That should be a snap for any kid with a pole barn in the back yard, but it still takes coaxing. Experts tell us that these life-lengthening activities should be divvied up into three categories: aerobic activity, muscle-strengthening exercises, and bone-strengthening exercises. No pediatricians have yet signed off on our workout, but that's no reason not to get your wee ones sweating the redneck way.

GET AEROBIC In more urbanized environments, children have access to family-life centers with trainer-led Zumba sessions and special classes where you get to ride fancy bicycles to nowhere. Redneck kids had better get the yard mowed before Mama gets home, or they'll wish they had somewhere safe to run.

BUILD MUSCLE In town, you can book an hour at a climbing gym for only $25, and the monkey bars over at Kidz Place feature bold and distinctive colors that help balance left brain/right brain neural pathways. In the boonies, those sacks of feed have to get in the barn before you can even think about jumping your mini-bike across the creek.

STRENGTHEN BONES City kids join skip-rope teams and train for 5k road races as a means of beefing up young femurs and vertebrae (while also establishing healthy peer relationships in non-individualized competitions). Redneck kids have fewer options, but seeing who can jump the farthest from the mule-shed roof has got to be good for young knees and ankles.

173 TEACH A KID TO DRIVE A STICK

Only about 5 percent of today's new vehicles come with a manual transmission, so it would seem that teaching a kid to drive a stick would be an obsolete skill. It's not.

Let's say your boy knocks on his prom date's door and shakes her dad's hand. "She's getting ready, son," he says. "How would like to escort my princess to prom in my old Vette?"

Your son can fumble around, Googling "how to drive a straight shift" on his phone before conceding, "No, I'll stick to my mom's van."

Or he can say, "Thank you, sir," before jumping into the driver's seat and burning through all six gears before they get to the end of the street. The old man might be left wondering which room in his house will be his new grandchild's—but he'll be impressed nonetheless.

Knowing how to drive a stick is critical to the self-reliant redneck lifestyle. Just teach using something old that won't be ruined by a few dents (I learned on an '80s model Toyota 4-Runner that I drove straight into a tree. I was 12).

Start on a very slight downhill slope, preferably on a gravel back road with minimal traffic, where the kid has the best chance to get the vehicle going. Have the engine running, gear in neutral, and parking brake set. Adjust the seat properly for your kid's legs. Let them get the feel of the clutch a few times before shifting to first gear. Have your kid slowly release the clutch and, just as the vehicle begins to move, give it just a bit of gas. The engine will die a few times, but laughing at that is just a part of the process.

Once the kid masters getting the vehicle going from a stop, teach him or her how to move through a couple gears—but you shouldn't go much over 30 miles per hour. The kid should master the feel of the clutch and getting the vehicle to start and stop without dying before gaining much speed—especially before moving on to the blacktop.

You *can* drive a stick, right? This should be easy. —W.B.

174 WATCH OUT FOR ROCKS

When I was 8, my dad and I were standing on the banks of the Jacks Fork River, skipping rocks. My little brother, Matt, who was 4, picked up a golf-ball-sized chunk of creek gravel and yelled, "Try this 'un, daddy!" He hurled it as hard as he could, and it smashed against Dad's temple from about 5 feet away. Pop crumpled to his knees, and Matt wailed in terror thinking he'd killed Dad for sure. (He hadn't—after a Busch Light, Dad was fine.)

Training redneck children to do much of anything is never without risk, but skipping rocks can be especially hazardous. Limit the lessons to one child at a time. Always stand behind the little devil. And until the child masters his or her technique, and learns the benefits of using a fairly small, flat rock, do most of the rock searching yourself.—W.B.

175 TEACH A KID TO BACK A TRAILER

From hauling lumber to towing a U-Haul to dropping a boat in the lake, understanding how to back a trailer is an essential skill that's best mastered early. Here are some tips to teach it the right way to a new driver.

GO BIG Obviously, the pupil should have mastered driving by now. Hook up a trailer and head to a big, empty parking lot. The Baptist church on Saturday is perfect.

SET SOME CONES Orange road cones won't tear up anything if you hit them, and you can use them to build a mock driveway or boat ramp.

USE THE MIRRORS The fastest way to learn to back a trailer is by looking over your shoulder. But trailers can be difficult to see from the driver's seat of some vehicles (especially big SUVs) by doing that. And once you learn that way, it's difficult to break the habit. Train your kid to back with the mirrors from the start.

GO ONE WHEEL AT A TIME Teach the kid to use the driver-side mirror as his primary reference mirror for lining up the trailer. The passenger-side mirror is just for double-checking progress and correcting errors.

TAKE IT SLOW Once your kid understands the fundamentals of where the trailer will go upon turning the steering wheel left or right, the key is to take it slow. If the vehicle you're using will move the trailer at idle speed, stick to that at first.

COOKING & DRINKING

Rednecks don't cook just so they can just share pictures of their dinner on Facebook. To us, food and drink should taste good, fill the gut, and perhaps liven the conversation.

It shouldn't cost much money, either, since we can kill or grow most of the ingredients ourselves.

Rednecks don't really use garnish, but that doesn't mean our recipes are going to be universally simple. No one ever made deer jerky correctly and said, "Well, that was easy." Some of the best whiskey out there has been carefully aged for months through a very specific process and is distilled so purely that it ends up as clear as water. Then, it's sipped from a communal mason jar to liven any conversation. —W.B.

176 OPEN A BEER WITH ANYTHING

The one time I asked my buddy Hartwell if he had a knife I could borrow, he replied with a sneer, "Am I wearing pants?" Lesson learned. Same with leaving the house without a church key. But like turning the ATV over in the field ditch when you were putting a dip in, it happens, so every 'neck needs to know at least a couple ways to MacGyver open a beer.

TRY BLADE WORK Hold the neck of the beer bottle tightly, with the top of your hand just under the bottom of the cap. Place the back of a knife blade across the top of the third knuckle of your index finger, and wedge it under the edge of the cap. Then, pry the spine of the blade up—carefully. Very carefully.

DRINK FOR A DOLLAR Fold the dollar bill in half, crease the fold, and roll the bill up as tightly as you can, then fold the rolled bill in half. Crook your index finger and place the rolled bill on top, with the fold barely sticking over the edge of your finger. Hold it in place with your thumb. Hold the bottle tightly with your other hand. Place the fold of the bill under the cap and push upward with the bill.

UNLOCK YOUR BREW Hold the beer bottle tightly, and place the tip of a key under one of the concave folds in the bottle cap. Pry the key to bend the fold outward. Bend out two or three neighboring folds. Insert the tip of the key under the worked edge of the cap, and pry it off. —T.E.N.

177 PAIR YOUR BEERS RIGHT

Whatever it is you're doing, there's a right beer in the right place at the right time. Take a look at our taste pairing suggestions.

YOU JUST . . .	YOU'RE DRINKING . . .	WITH HINTS OF . . .
Pushed your truck back into the shed. The alternator failed after only 273,422 miles, and now it's time to fix it.	Miller High Life	Champagne, dielectric grease, and overdraft fees. This is the beer of mechanical triumphs.
Left the tanning bed and dyed your hair "trailer park Barbie" blonde for the summer. Dang, girl.	Bud Light Lime	Citrus and skin cancer. If ever there were a beer for dancing on a pontoon boat, this is it.
Finished cutting up a winter's worth of firewood. You're not wearing a flannel shirt and boots for the irony.	Pabst Blue Ribbon	Two-stroke mix, sawdust, and confusion. Why is that other logger at the end of the bar wearing women's jeans?
Dumped 25 pounds of boiled crustaceans, taters, and assorted sausages onto a table that was used only last week for cleaning catfish. Newspaper sanitizes good as bleach.	Coors Light— several of them	A unique blend of Creole seasoning and mountain spring water, since the brew of the Rockies flows cold and proud, straight downhill to Louisiana.
Strung the last of the Christmas lights and put some bells around the neck of your 10-point shoulder mount. The family will be over in a bit.	Budweiser	Cream and celebration. You wouldn't normally drink a beer this nice, but it is Jesus's birthday.

178 MAKE A BEER CAP FISHING LURE

As a little crafting project, go on and open a bottle of beer, make this fishing lure, and catch a fish in less time that it will take for the beer to get warm. That's good living.

STEP 1 Using pliers, flatten the sides of the bottle cap, then bend in half.

STEP 2 Place a split shot into the fold for a bit of rattle, and use pliers to seal the edges. Pretty good is good enough.

STEP 3 Place the lure body on a spare piece of wood. Use a hammer and small nail to pierce a hole in each end, close to the edge of the metal.

STEP 4 Thread a split ring into one hole, and slip a treble hook onto the split ring. Add a quick-release swivel to the other hole.

STEP 5 Tie to your line, and cast!

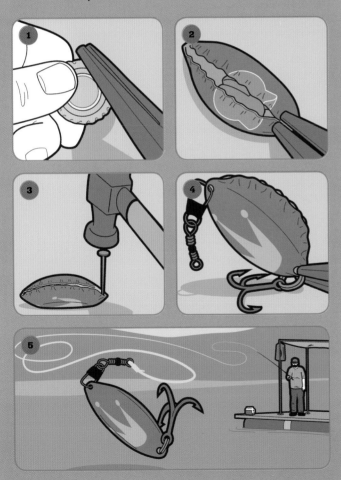

179 TEACH A DOG TO FETCH A BEER

You can train your duck dog to fetch a cold beer from the fridge, which conveniently enough, pairs perfectly with a grilled mallard. You need a dedicated beer fridge, a piece of rope, and the patience for repetitive drills. Your dog should've already mastered basic obedience commands and be trained to fetch before attempting to teach him or her this trick.

STOCK THE FRIDGE You doubtless already have a beer fridge in your shop, so this part is easy. Just in case you haven't made this investment yet, you need a fridge full of beer on a shelf that's low enough for the dog to reach.

ROPE IT OFF Tie a piece of rope to the fridge handle. First train the dog to grab the rope, and then gradually progress to pulling open the door, rewarding progress with praise or a treat. You'll need to work on a command, too, like, "Bowser, get Daddy a pork chop!" Simply saying, "get a beer" works, too. Repeat this enough so that the dog understands that when he opens the fridge, good things will result.

GRAB A COLD ONE With the fridge open, encourage the dog to take a beer in his mouth while giving the command—and reward his progress. Next, take a few steps back, and tell the dog bring the beer to hand, using the same command you'd use to get him to deliver anything else. With practice, a young retriever will master the beer fetch in a surprisingly short time—and it's a trick guaranteed to outshine *sit, shake,* or *pee on that tire*.

180 ASK FOR LEMONADE

In some deep mountain holler, a delicious secret is being aged in an oak barrel. The recipe is precise, but it isn't written down. Instead, it's been passed via word of mouth through the generations. Some old timers guarded it with shotguns and a willingness to serve hard time.

The legalities of sipping this special brew are murky. Technically, probably, it's illegal—but since judges and sheriffs seem to like it well as anyone, having a jar in your spice cabinet isn't high on the worry list.

Still, you don't go asking for it, especially if you're not from around here. Polite craftsmen will simply say no, and point out that plenty of stores sell what you're after. Old timers might threaten to beat the snot out of you.

Play it cool. Take your time. Get to know people. And never ask for it by name. What you'd like is a little lemonade or some of that good mountain spring water, and you've heard so-and-so has the best around. Play your cards right, and you just might be given directions to a special hollowed-out stump deep in the woods.

181 MAKE STRAWBERRY SCHNAPPS

This concoction starts out sweeter than a Blow-Pop, but in time, it matures into a deep-red sipping drink. Use fully ripe berries, and don't skimp on the booze; you'll need at least 80 proof since the berries contain so much water. There's less water in wild strawberries, so the schnapps will pack more punch.

STEP 1 Pick, clean, and wash the berries. Cut off the caps, and place them on paper towels in the shade to dry thoroughly.

STEP 2 Fill a glass jug two-thirds with berries, then fill the rest with high-test vodka. Cap tightly.

STEP 3 Store in a cool, shady place. You can dip into it after a couple weeks, but it's much better aged a minimum of 4 months. Turn the bottle a few times to mix it, and then strain the liquid through cheesecloth into a clean glass jar.

182 HAVE A BLACK-PAN SPA DAY

We've all been guilty of it at one time or another, but it's a special kind of sorry that makes a person clean a cast iron pan or Dutch oven poorly, letting that well-seasoned, non-stick layer of goodness turn to crud and rust. Thankfully, a black pan has a pure heart, and will forgive such shameful treatment in return for a little love, care, and elbow grease. Here's how to bring cast iron back from the dead.

STEP 1 Scrape off loose bits of old seasoning, burned-on food scraps, and the despicable rust and general funk. Preheat the oven to 350 degrees. Scrub the pan with hot soapy water, repeating to yourself that this is the last time soapy water will touch the pan. Rinse thoroughly, then dry in the oven for 10 minutes.

STEP 2 Remove the pan from the oven, let cool, and pour a quarter-cup of liquid oil and a cup of coarse kosher salt into the middle of the pan. Using a clean cotton rag, work the oil and salt into the pan, adding more as needed. Scrub inside and out, and be meticulous around the rusty spots.

STEP 3 Rinse off the pan and give it a second good scrubbing, this time using a solution of a cup of white vinegar to a quart of water. Rust, crud, and loose seasoning should now have vanished, showing bare metal where the new seasoning will be applied. Rinse and dry in the oven for 10 minutes.

STEP 4 Remove the pan from the oven and let it cool enough to handle. Work a thin layer of shortening all over the pan, inside and out—lids, handles, everything. Back in the oven it goes, upside down, for an hour. Remove the pan, and let it cool. Wipe away excess grease that has pooled in the bottom—then give it another round: more shortening and another hour-long stint in the oven.

183 SKIP THE SUPERMARKET

Want to put together a redneck repast? Look no further than your own backwoods for plenty of good eatin'.

THE WILD STUFF	HOW TO GET IT	WHAT TO MAKE
Morel mushrooms emerge after the first few warm spring rains, just about the time oak leaves are sprouting.	Look for morels on sunny, well-drained hillsides, often near sycamore and poplar trees. Smaller black morels emerge first; larger yellow morels come on a week or two later. Cut them in half lengthwise, and wash them thoroughly.	Sauté morels and serve alongside a good venison steak, or dip them in batter and deep-fry them. Big-city chefs pay a pretty penny for morel mushrooms, but if you know where to look, you can bring home buckets full for free.
Ramps are a wild onion with a serious garlic punch. Legend holds that old Appalachian schools had separate classrooms for pungent ramp eaters in the spring.	Look near creeks in rich, moist hardwood soil. Use a trowel or hoe to get the bulbs out of the ground; leave some to seed next year's crop. Wash off the dirt, peel off the outer thin skin, and cut off the end of the root.	Like onions, ramps can be grilled, roasted, sautéed, and eaten raw. For an Appalachian classic, stuff a fresh trout with ramps and butter, and pan sauté or cook in foil on a campfire.
Blackberries begin to ripen in early summer, and there's good picking for a couple weeks after the first ones get sweet.	Leave the green and red berries alone for a few more days; focus on the darkest ones you can find, which are deliciously sweet. But watch out—the vines are covered in briars and, very often, ticks.	Despite the seeds, blackberries are pretty good straight off the vine—but the Holy Grail of summer desserts is cobbler with a good scoop of whipped cream.
Sassafras makes a great tea and a pretty good licorice stick. The small tree grows practically everywhere.	It's easy to identify—leaves on the small tree have three different shapes: single, double, and triple lobes. Pull up knee- to waist-high saplings, and clean and skin the roots.	Chew on a skinned root for a licorice bite. Or fray a green twig for a DIY toothbrush. For sassafras tea, steep cleaned roots in water, strain, and sweeten.
Smooth and staghorn **sumac** berries produce a tart drink, like Kool-Aid gone wild.	Look for ripe summer berry clusters in open sun, but pick before heavy rains dilute the potency. After collecting, check for spiders, bugs, and other hitchhikers.	Place 6–8 clusters in a pitcher and add a half-gallon of cold water. Use your hands to rub off the red layer that has most of the flavoring. Steep for up to 2 hours; taste occasionally to monitor tartness. Strain through cheesecloth or a clean pillowcase. Add maple syrup, honey, or sugar to taste.
Persimmons are the largest native berry in the country, and trees are heavy with the fruits in the fall.	Pick a persimmon too early and the astringent fruit will pucker your mouth inside out. The fruits are ripe when you can shake them out of the tree.	Eat them raw, or skin and push them through a colander to pulp the flesh, and make jelly, bread, pancakes, and syrup. Frozen pulp is a poor man's ice cream.

184 BREW MUSCADINE WINE

There are as many recipes for homemade muscadine wine as there are for hunter's stew, squirrel pie, or any other dish with a heritage dating back to the flintlock era. This one comes from Cajun humorist Gene Buller, for whom making the best of whatever comes out of his beloved Louisiana woods was no laughing matter. Once bottled, this wine will keep for years—but it won't last a month once folks hear it's ready.

Ingredients

1 gallon muscadines

3 gallons distilled water

1 package yeast (not rapid rise)

8 pounds sugar

Crush the muscadines in a plastic bag, or place them in a freezer until the skins burst. (Wear rubber gloves while crushing muscadines—they are highly acidic.) Combine the crushed fruit with distilled water and yeast in a clean 5-gallon bucket. Stir well. Cover and let stand for 24 hours. Strain the pulp by pouring the mixture through a double layer of cheesecloth into a second clean 5-gallon bucket. Stir in the sugar until it's dissolved.

Carefully pour the mixture into clean jugs. Top the mouths of the jugs with triple layers of cheesecloth held in place with rubber bands. The fermenting juice will bubble and foam like carbonated water for up to nine weeks. When the mixture quits bubbling, wait 2 days, then transfer the wine into glass bottles with screw caps.

185 MAKE CAMP BISCUITS

A good biscuit fills a belly, sops up the last of the bacon grease, and will bear up pretty well during a half-day ride in your front pocket. Making camp biscuits can be as involved as building them from scratch, or as easy as busting open a can and daring your buddies to say a word. Here's the DIY route.

STEP 1 Mix 2 cups flour, 3 teaspoons baking powder, and 1 teaspoon salt.

STEP 2 Using a fork, cut ¼ cup of vegetable shortening into the mix until it has a crumbly texture.

STEP 3 Add ¾ cup buttermilk and 3 tablespoons orange juice.

STEP 4 Fold the mixture over itself until it forms a dough.

STEP 5 Cut biscuits with a jelly jar, the way God intended.

187 GET TO THE HEART OF IT

The first deer of the season is something to celebrate, whether at home or in deer camp. This recipe is a nod to age-old traditions of dining on venison heart as a symbolic gesture of thanks.

Ingredients

Heart and liver from the season's first deer

4 beef bouillon cubes

½ pound bacon

3 onions, chopped

3 cups flour

½ cup dry red wine

Vegetable oil, if needed.

With a very sharp knife, slice the heart and liver into ½-inch-thick slices. Rinse and drain. Dredge the slices through flour, and set aside. Cook the bacon, and remove from drippings.

Brown the heart and liver slices in bacon grease, adding vegetable oil if needed. Remove the heart and liver slices, and set them aside; add onions, and brown.

Crumble bacon into the pan, then add the heart and liver slices. Add beef bouillon cubes, wine, and enough water to cover. Simmer 30 minutes, stirring occasionally to mix the bouillon. Thicken the gravy with flour if desired.

Serve over rice or mashed potatoes.

186 WHIP UP RED-EYE GRAVY

This Southern deer camp staple turns ham drippings and coffee into the elixir of the swamp gods.

Ingredients

Slow-cook or 5-minute grits (never instant grits), prepared according to directions on the package.

2 servings country ham

¼ to ½ cup strong coffee

1 teaspoon vegetable oil

7-Up

Grease a cast iron or aluminum pan with vegetable oil. Fry the ham for 2 to 3 minutes per side. Add a few tablespoons of 7-Up and stir; the sugar in the soda will caramelize, and help the ham stick to the pan. Stir and scrape all the drippings from the bottom of the pan. Remove the ham from the pan.

Add the coffee to the drippings. Heat until just below boiling for 2 minutes, constantly stirring and scraping. Add the ham back to the skillet; stir to reheat thoroughly. Spoon your red-eye gravy over grits.

188 KNOW YOUR GAS STATION CUISINE

Rednecks have a special bond with gas station food. It keeps us on the go when we're behind the wheel, and the best of it finds its way into blind bags, tackle boxes, and deer stand daypacks. There are some cautionary articles out there about the unhealthiness of gas station snacks—this isn't one of them.

FUNYUNS These are the best gun-range snack ever. If you can keep three shots inside a Funyun ring, you're ready to shoot a deer.

CRISPITOS Should you have the great fortune to even find a Crispito, it will likely have aged for a few hours under a heat lamp. Don't worry—aged Crispitos are the best ones.

SUNFLOWER SEEDS Made specifically for rednecks trying to quit chewing tobacco, sunflower seeds even allow for use of your favorite spittoon.

GRANOLA BARS Not that anyone actually likes eating these, but even after a couple years in a blind bag, granola bars are still technically edible.

HEAT-RACK SAUSAGE These rotisserie sirens, glowing under the heat lamp, almost dare you to eat them just before daylight, when you're far from the nearest bathroom.

POWDERED MINI DONUTS The sugary coating doubles as a good wind-checker, in case you're about to stalk a critter or set something afire.

189 MAKE SOME JERKY

Jerky is good for road trips, snacking in the deer stand, and stocking up for the collapse of society. It's easiest to make from lean red meat (fat adds moisture content), and it's a great way to use up extra "stuff," like venison trimmings and shoulders. It's an outstanding use of a pile of goose breasts, too.

PREP IT Sliced jerky is easiest to make. Use a sharp fillet knife to cut the meat across the grain, keeping the strips relatively uniform in size and thickness. Ground jerky is good, too—and the finished product tends to be a bit more consistent. I use a jerky gun (which looks like a caulk gun) to make ground jerky strips. Whether you are using sliced or ground meat, be sure to weigh it prior to seasoning. Knowing how much raw meat you're preparing allows you to know how much seasoning and cure to use from the kit or how to repeat the recipe down the road if you're mixing your own.

CURE IT Not every jerky chef uses curing salt, but it adds an extra safety measure if you're storing jerky for any length of time. You can order the salt in bulk (it's easy to find online), but most jerky kits come with enough curing salt for 5 to 10 pounds of raw meat. Mix both the salt and cure in a bit of cold water, and season the meat a few pounds at a time. Mix it well, then allow your meat to chill overnight.

DRY IT Jerky can be dried in the oven on low heat with the door propped open, in a smoker (sans the liquid pan), or in a dehydrator. You want it dry but not crispy, bendable but not greasy. Allow it to cool, then store it in the refrigerator or freezer in zip-top or vacuum-sealed bags. —W.B.

190 BOIL MUD BUGS

You don't have to live in Louisiana to have a crawfish boil, but you do have to enjoy eating from a newspaper-covered table with your hands. Like that's a problem.

GET THE BUGS If you live in the Deep South, getting crawfish is as easy as stopping by the seafood market in spring. In the Mid-South, seasonal trucks will sell bugs (though they cost a bit). Farther north, you'll have to pay through the nose to overnight them, or buy them frozen in the grocery store.

PURGE 'EM OUT The proper way to "purge" crawfish of dirt and impurities (a.k.a. poop) is a subject of great debate among Cajun chefs. Some swear a saltwater bath helps loosen crawfish bowels; others stick to cool, fresh water. Some say purging kills perfectly good crawfish—and if there's one rule of a crawfish boil, it's to throw out the dead ones. At the least, wash live crawdads in cold water (salt is optional) to get the gunk from the shells.

PREPARE THE BOIL Plan for about 3 pounds of crawfish per person. Not everyone eats the full three pounds, but some might eat four. A 5-gallon stock pot holds 6 to 7 pounds of crawfish, plus all the fixings. Prepare a seafood boil (disclosure: I use Old Bay seafood boil), and add garlic, Cajun seasoning, red pepper, salt, and whatever else you like; followed with potatoes and onions. Boil for 15 minutes, add sliced Andouille sausage and corn on the cob, and then boil another 15 minutes.

ADD THE BUGS Add the crawfish (frozen bugs should be at least partly thawed first), and once the water returns to boiling, pour in at least a half cup of white vinegar, to help the meat pop out of the shells. Boil the bugs for 15 minutes (until bright red), turn off the heat, cover the pot, and let it sit for 20 or 30 minutes. Drain the water from the pot, pour the whole mess out on the table, let it cool for half a beer, then dig in. —W.B.

DON'T BURN DOWN THE DORM

On my last night as a Murray State University student, days before my wedding, Matt Seymore and I set the dormitory kitchen on fire.

It was mid-May, and Seymore, who'd just finished up at the University of Louisville, had driven in to go bluegill fishing with me. By sunset, we had forty big bream on ice.

Finals were over, so the dorm was mostly vacant, save for a few holdouts like me, and the squad of residential advisors. One of the RAs was Michelle Adams—my fiancé—and she'd written me up a few days prior because I'd thrown away a mattress pad supplied by Murray State.

"I wasn't sleeping on that thing," I told her. "It was disgusting, and besides, we're getting married in like a week. Can't you cut me a break?"

"No," she said with a slight grin. "Here's your citation."

The $35 I'd been forced to pay Murray State for a crusty mattress pad was fresh on my mind when Seymore and I pulled into the parking lot with fish to clean. We'd already bought the cornmeal, frozen French fries, and vegetable oil.

"What we ought to do," Seymore said as he honed his fillet knife against a steel, "is have us a little whiskey while we cut up these fish." I agreed.

I swaddled a two-thirds-full bottle of Early Times in a towel, past the front desk, where Michelle was working, and into the parking lot. Seymore and I only needed an hour and a bit of the whiskey to finish the fish.

The community kitchen was just down the hall from Michelle's front desk post. We had one single 12-inch, cast iron skillet for frying 80 fillets, along with 2 pounds of frozen fries.

As the pile of golden fillets grew higher, Seymore and I continued our progress on the bottle. "Man," I said, leaning against the counter. "We ought to finish dinner before I have any more."

Seymore shook a few of the frozen fries into the grease, where they popped and sizzled. "Fill that skillet up!" I said, taking the bag from his hands and ripping it open. The remaining fries rolled into the skillet in a frozen wad. Oil sloshed onto the burner, and the stovetop erupted into a ball of flames.

Seymore grabbed the open bag of corn meal and dumped it onto the element as I shut off the burner. The meal extinguished the flame, but seared into black sludge that sent smoke billowing through the dorm. The fire alarm rang; we heard students scramble and scream down the stairs and through the smoke.

Michelle appeared before us, trembling with anger, like a little specter in the smoke. "The fire department is on its way," she sneered.

"Well, the fire's already out!" I said defiantly. The stove was still billowing smoke as if hit by a meteorite. Seymore grabbed the whiskey bottle and had a little nip. Michelle's gaze tightened.

The fire truck arrived, lights flashing and siren wailing. Six uniformed men marched inside, and Michelle happily directed them toward me.

Two industrial fans were needed to purge all the smoke from the dorm. As far as I know, the place still smells of it.

"Danged if those firemen didn't eat every fillet of fish we had," Seymore said after they left. We ordered pizza.

Five days later in a little church, Seymore stood as a groomsmen as Michelle and I said our vows. —W.B.

GUNS & KNIVES

Firearms have been major symbols of self-reliance since North America was settled, and if you take nothing else from this book, you should know that rednecks prefer to take care of themselves. Show us a crisis, and we'll do our best to fix it—but we're going to arm ourselves first. Knowing how to safely and effectively handle a gun is the single most important redneck skill there is to learn.

Other tools, particularly good knives, can capture a redneck's attention, especially if we're in possession of a tax refund. You might think that you'll never need a Bowie knife of your own, but if you ever find yourself fighting it out with an enraged bear, like Brandon Johnson did with his eight-dollar knife (see #61), you'll be thankful for a big blade. Probably, you'll wish it was just a touch bigger. And that it fired bullets. —W.B.

191 BUILD YOUR KNIFE COLLECTION

No self-respecting redneck would own just a single knife, not when there's all kinds of things that need cutting, carving, whittling, prying open, and slashing into a couple pieces or three. Here, in no particular order, are the five required blades for rednecks. If you're missing one, get to the hardware store pronto.

HAWKBILL A curving hawkbill knife is made for many redneck tasks, like cutting old carpet samples to fit the floor of your deer stand or pruning vines off the tractor shed. But mostly, the thing just looks so dang wicked it seems to say, "I have a bad day every day, so mind your own stinking business."

BUTTERFLY KNIFE Also known as the "balisong," the butterfly knife is a folder with roots in the Philippines. It sports two handles that rotate around the tang as the knife is opened with one hand. They are favored by actors in kung fu movies and pimply-faced teenagers who think they are as tough as actors in kung fu movies.

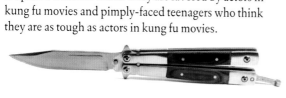

BUCK 110 Once upon a time it seemed that every pair of boot-cut blue jeans came standard with a Buck 110 in the pocket. Introduced in 1964, the iconic folder has a clip-point blade, a Macassar ebony handle, and high-gloss brass bolsters. Buck 110s are equally adept at skinning deer, cutting birthday cake, and cleaning toenails. Typically the only cleaning required between each of those tasks is a good lick and a wipe on a flannel shirt tail.

BOOT KNIFE It doesn't much matter which style or brand, as long as it clips to the upper shaft of a boot and can be deployed as quickly as you can pull up the leg of your pants and reach down there and get it. Never mind the fact that your opponent is already swinging the fat end of a pool cue at your head—boot knives exude cool.

ORIGINAL LEATHERMAN
The first Leatherman multi-tool came out in 1983 and launched a tsunami of copycats and knockoffs that hasn't yet abated. Those early Leathermans came in a brown leather sheath that still rides the belts of the best tow-truck operators, logging truck drivers, and outboard mechanics around.

192 KNOW THE BOWIE KNIFE

It was good enough for Jim Bowie, Rambo, and Crocodile Dundee, so surely the Bowie knife is good enough, plain and simple. Supposedly designed after a nasty fight on a Mississippi sandbar in 1827, the Bowie knife is a fixture of American cutlery. Today's knives evolved from whatever Bowie used to literally split a few heads back then, but the original had to be a doozy. One historian wrote: "It must be long enough to use as a sword, sharp enough to use as a razor, wide enough to use as a paddle, and heavy enough to use as a hatchet." Here are the most recognized elements of a Bowie knife— although Jim himself might disagree.

FIXED BLADE (A) Built for strength, up to 9 inches long. The U.S. Marine Corps KA-BAR fighting and utility knife, shown here, was introduced for World War II as a shortened Bowie with a 7-inch blade.

SWEEPING CLIP POINT (B) This shape is intended for greater stabbing penetration, although the original Bowie likely had a straight spine.

FALSE EDGE (C) This feature can usually be sharpened for a wicked back-handed slash. It can make a mess of cleaning a deer, though.

DOUBLE QUILLON (D) Also simply known as the handguard or crossguard. You wouldn't want your hand slipping onto that huge blade, after all, would you?

193 CRAFT A PVC RIFLE REST

One of the worst feelings in life is the one you get when a 3-pound fox squirrel moves just beyond the point where you feel comfortable shooting without a rest, and you can't do a thing but watch a solid quart of Brunswick stew slip through the woods. Never feel that pain again with this PVC rifle rest.

Glue a 4-inch piece of 1¼-inch PVC pipe into the branch of a T-joint (1), and pad it with black foam or camouflage tape (2). In the field, cut a 1-inch-thick sapling about 4 feet long. Slip the T-joint over the stick (3) so the padded branch juts off to the side—there's your mini shooting rail. To aim, grasp the stick and pipe at the proper level, cradle the rifle in the rest, and feed your family.

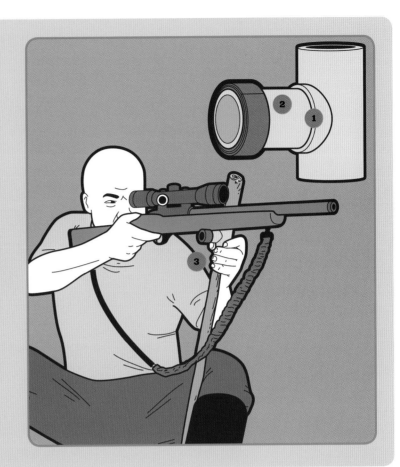

194 TURN A PISTOL INTO A SHOTGUN

Ranchers in serious snake country are known for toting revolvers loaded with rat shot for those too-close encounters with Mr. No Shoulders. There are plenty of myths and misinformation about shotshells for handguns, so here's what you need to know.

MICRO SHOT Pistol shotshells are loaded with tiny shot. In .22 and .22 Magnum, most shells are filled with tiny #11 or #12 shot. Step up to the larger calibers—9mm, .38, .40, .44, .45—and the shot size can creep up to #9. That's still pretty lightweight stuff, but it'll do the trick.

BARREL BASHING It's a misconception that shooting rat shot in a rifled barrel will ruin the barrel. Lead shot won't damage a steel barrel. Shoot a lot of the stuff, however, and lead and plastic fouling could be an issue, so clean barrels with a bronze brush after taking a shot.

SEMI-AUTO PAINS Plastic-encased rat shot is a questionable load for semi-automatic pistols. Even if it does cycle, there's a chance that the feed ramp or another metal part might tear the plastic cap and allow spilled lead shot to dump into the inner workings of your handgun. That's no good.

BOTTOM LINE Rat shot from these calibers is a short-range, tiny-game load. The shot cups spin from the rifling, so the pattern opens quickly, and the shot itself is too small to do much damage. They're great for bumblebees on the wing, blackbirds at 20 feet, and rats, mice, and snakes at point-blank ranges. Not ideal for something as tough as a squirrel, though.

195 SIGHT IN ON THE CHEAP

You don't need a whole box of shells to zero a rifle. If you're cheap, and good, you can do it in three shots.

You'll need a friend to help, and a rifle that will print on the target. Here's the drill.

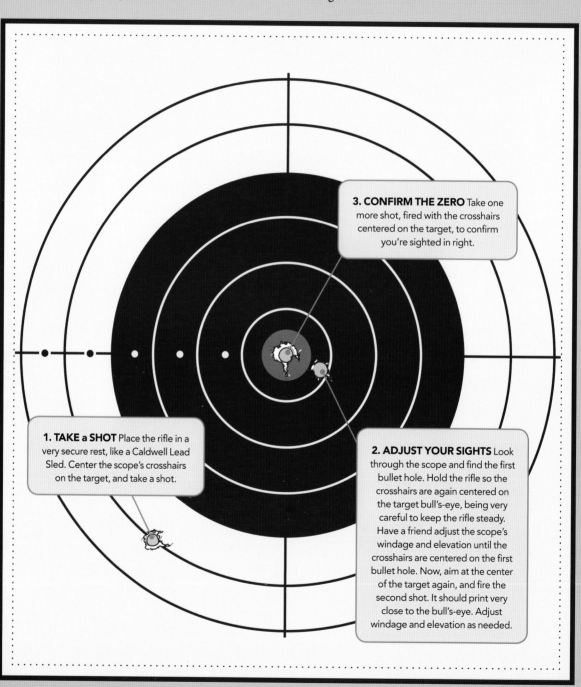

3. CONFIRM THE ZERO Take one more shot, fired with the crosshairs centered on the target, to confirm you're sighted in right.

1. TAKE a SHOT Place the rifle in a very secure rest, like a Caldwell Lead Sled. Center the scope's crosshairs on the target, and take a shot.

2. ADJUST YOUR SIGHTS Look through the scope and find the first bullet hole. Hold the rifle so the crosshairs are again centered on the target bull's-eye, being very careful to keep the rifle steady. Have a friend adjust the scope's windage and elevation until the crosshairs are centered on the first bullet hole. Now, aim at the center of the target again, and fire the second shot. It should print very close to the bull's-eye. Adjust windage and elevation as needed.

196 THROW A KNIFE

I still have the scar on my thigh where my brother, Mark, stuck me with his knife while we were playing with our new blades at a campground in the Great Smokies. I must have been 10 or 11 years old, and as blood gushed over the seat of my daddy's Ford Pinto station wagon—the fancy upgrade, with the fake wood down the side—I learned first-hand why you should never play with a knife. That's not to say you can't throw one. Should you ever want to hurl a blade—away from your brother—here's the drill.

STEP 1 Start about 4 feet from a tree. Hold the knife by the spine of the blade, with the edge facing away so you don't cut your hand.

STEP 2 Keep your wrist stiff throughout the throwing motion.

STEP 3 You'll use the same speed and motion for each throw, so take note of the knife's rotation it the air, and adjust your distance so it hits the target point-first.

STEP 4 Once you have one-and-half rotations down pat, increase your distance. —T.E.N.

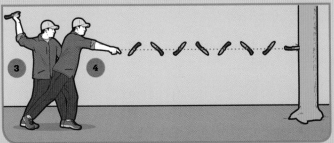

197 UP YOUR PLINKING GAME

When old farts went plinking, they shot pine cones and knotholes in tree stumps. These days, it's pretty easy to dial up the fun with a bunch of reactive targets from the Mart of Wall. Here's what to toss in the cart next time you're at the store, plus other fun things to whack with a .22.

ANIMAL CRACKERS They're cheap, and environmentally friendly to boot.

EGGS Another fun thing to blow up that won't explode the wallet.

FLOUR Pin a bag to a good backstop, and blast at long range.

KOOL-AID ICE CUBES Kids love to make them—and shoot them.

BABY CARROTS Wedge these into tree branches, then shoot on a walk through the woods.

CHEAP SODA Blowout-sale soda is always a winner.

CONDIMENT PACKETS Load up on extra packets on your next burger joint visit. Pin to a backstop and splatterize.

CHARCOAL BRIQUETTES A center shot turns them into a black puffball.

FIGURINES Hit the local flea market for cheap, used fast-food toys.

PLAYING CARDS Line 'em up for a game of rimfire blackjack.

POKER CHIPS Brightly colored, thus easy to see if you score from 100 yards.

PAINTBALLS Pulverize leftover ammo from your last paintball showdown.

198 DO MORE WITH DUCT TAPE

Where there is duct tape, there is life. Just ask the astronauts of Apollo 17, who used it to rig a fender extension on a lunar module that was kicking up too much moon dust. True story. There are a lot of cheap duct tapes out there, so stick with the best: 3M or genuine Duck Tape. If you want to ratchet up the adhesion, Gorilla Tape is serious business, but it doesn't come cheap. —T.E.N.

START A FIRE Fresh out of dried bird nests, tinder fungus, and cattail fluff? Loosely wad up an orange-sized orb of duct tape and light with a match. You'll have a towering eight-minute inferno.

MAKE EMERGENCY SPLINTS Your health insurance probably won't approve, but duct tape, and popsicle sticks or the plastic from spent shotgun shells or empty soda bottles, can be used to fashion backwoods splints for fingers and wrists.

PROTECT YOUR PRIVATES Ticks and chiggers love your most tender parts. Keep 'em out by tightly taping the cuffs of your pant legs around your ankles.

REMOVE INSECTS If you neglect to tape your britches, the sticky side of duct tape is the best device for quickly removing chiggers and tiny "seed" ticks that have yet to dig in. Prepare to lose some hair as collateral damage.

MAKE A BOWL A half-acre of blackberries and no way to tote them home? Sit down, bend a knee, and wrap tape around it until you have a basket. Remove it, turn it inside out, slip the bowl back over your knee, and cover the sticky side with another layer. Now you're ready to load up.

TEND BLISTERS Ignore hot spots and they'll only get worse. At the first sign of burning pain, cover the spot with duct tape. Its friction-shedding properties cannot be overstated. Round the corners to keep it from peeling off.

SET BUTTERFLY SUTURES In an emergency first-aid situation, deep cuts can be held together with duct tape. Cut a strip of tape about 1 inch by 2 inches. Cut a flap into each long side, and fold the flaps in to create an elongated H.

PATCH BOAT SEATS I blew out the old cane webbing on my canoe seat six years ago, but the duct tape field fix has lasted since. Remove the worn-out webbing, clean the seat frame with warm water and a mild detergent, and let dry. Run four layers of duct tape in a basket-weave pattern across the seat frame, leaving a ½-inch gap between each band of tape so water can drain.

199 GET MORE OUT OF PARACORD

Don't be fooled by cheap imitations. Real parachute cord, a.k.a. 550 cord, is a braided nylon sheath around seven to nine smaller interwoven strands. It has a minimum breaking strength of 550 pounds, and at least twice that number of uses. Here are ten of them.

RIG A SHOOTING RAIL After hoisting your gun into your treestand with your p-cord pull rope, tie off one end to the tree or stand, and toss the line over a limb above your seat. Tie a loop in the dangling end, using a taut-line hitch. You can adjust the height of this makeshift shooting rail by sliding the knot up or down the rope. When it's time to take a shot, thread your barrel through the loop.

TIE A GAME STRAP Halve a 10-foot length of cord, then halve it again. Tie an overhand knot in the middle. Cut the loops. Tie a sliding loop knot in the end of each of the eight tags. Each loop will hold a goose or several ducks, squirrels, or quail.

SET A TROTLINE Remove the inner strands from a length of paracord and use the outer sheath as your main trot line, with either end tied to a tree or sapling. Space the inner cords along the main line, and tie a hook to each, for drop lines.

HANG GAME When field dressing big game solo, roll the animal on its back, and tether a hind hoof to a stout sapling or tree, to hold the carcass still while you make that long belly incision.

FAKE A FIELD WRENCH Can't get a rusty bolt loose? Tightly wrap paracord, around the nut counterclockwise, leaving a tag end long enough to grasp firmly and pull.

MAKE DENTAL FLOSS Got something stuck in your teeth? Use inner cord as field floss.

BUILD A SURVIVAL BOLA Cut three 3-foot lengths of cord, and tie the ends together with a single overhand knot. Tie rocks or fabric pouches of stones to the free ends. For birds, use 6 to 8 strands.

DIVIDE YOUR TENT String up a ridgeline of paracord, and hang a poncho or space blanket, for privacy in a shared tent.

SLICE CHEESE Should you find yourself without a knife, use a section of inner cord to slice cheese and salami.

CUT THE CORD Tie a length of paracord that you want to cut to two stout points, leaving plenty of slack. Take another couple feet of cord and lay it over the length to be cut. Grasp each end of this second piece firmly, and saw back and forth. Friction will melt the paracord right where you want it cut.

ON THE FARM

My grandfather, who grew up during the Depression and was known to drive an extra 20 minutes to save 10 cents on a box of nails, once told me, "Buy a little piece of property soon as you're able. You'll never regret it."

Owning ground—and it doesn't have to be much—is the pinnacle of the redneck dream. It's a place you'll always have to hunt, fish, or shoot beer cans with your .45 while wearing flip-flops. Most of your time as a landowner will be spent taking care of the land, and nothing about that is easy. Then again, the work almost universally involves cussing, sweating, and some beer—the trifecta of redneck recreation—so maybe it's easier than it seems. —W.B.

200 GET A TRACTOR DEAL

A four-wheeler has its place for spreading fertilizer, but if you're serious about crops, get a tractor. Even my 16-horse Kubota B7100, which I bought used for $3,000, outdoes an ATV with more horsepower. I suggest a big tractor for long-term use, but a tight budget works with these rules.

BUY OLD Diesel tractors run forever with regular maintenance, so there are plenty of old ones for sale on Craigslist in rural areas. Tractorhouse.com is a good specialist site to shop for and price-check various models.

INSPECT IT A used tractor should start easily and run smoothly. The hydraulic system and power take off (PTO) should work. Grease fittings should be good and greasy. Minor rust and leaks are to be expected on old tractors, but anything more than that is a sign of neglect.

DO YOUR RESEARCH For some subcompact tractors, spare parts are near impossible to find, and old tractors inevitably break down on occasion, so avoid that class.

TILL IT UP Disk harrows require weight to cut soil, so small ones are limited, but most any tractor runs a rotary tiller, which powders the soil, creating a perfect bed for small seeds. A 15- to 25-horse tractor will handle most 48-inch and smaller tillers with ease. —W.B.

201 BURN IT DOWN

Prescribed fire is a great way to manage vegetation on a small farm. It kills invasive saplings and grasses, restores the native seedbed, and reduces wildfire risk by cleaning up duff and leaf litter.

GEAR UP Get safety gear, rakes, flappers, backpack sprayers with water, extra water tanks, and extra people. Drip torches work for starting a burn, but I've used pump sprayers, a mix of 75:25 diesel/gasoline, and a grill lighter.

PLAN THE DAY Study burn laws and requirements in your area, and only burn on days with optimal wind and humidity. I prefer 50 percent humidity and at least a 10-mph steady breeze to help carry the fire.

BACKFIRE FIRST Start a "backfire" on the downwind edge of the burn area, to burn steadily into the wind, and make a 4- to 5-foot-wide line of ash that the head fire cannot cross.

LIGHT THE HEAD FIRE With a good back-burn line established, start a few small fires or ignite a steady line upwind of the burn area. With a good wind, this fire will burn fast and hot until it meets the backfire.

INSPECT THE BURN With a good rain and warm weather, the area will green up within weeks. Insects, songbirds, turkeys, and deer will flourish in a newly burned area—that's exactly why you do it. —W.B.

202 BREAK IT UP

Before you set your place aflame, you must build suitable firebreaks. These crucial lanes of bare ground need to be twice the width of the anticipated flame height. If the vegetation you're planning to burn is 6 feet tall, you'll need a firebreak that's at least 12 feet wide. If you have a tractor with a tiller or disk,

you can probably build the firebreaks yourself (though in especially rough ground, it can be best to hire a dozer operator for a day to install them). Once firebreaks are built, you can maintain them for a lifetime, and even plant them with clover or other food-plot plants.

203 HOOK UP A 3-POINT IMPLEMENT ON YOUR OWN

The three-point linkage is the heart of a tractor's working potential. This system lets an implement attach to the tractor at (you guessed it) three points, instead of being pulled behind it. Two lower lift arms are powered by the tractor's hydraulics, and they attach to the implement with pins. The third link attaches at the top; it's threaded, to adjust the height and angle of the implement.

The first step in hooking up an implement is properly unhooking it. Set an implement in an area with plenty of room to maneuver, and ensure the ground is level before unhooking. If needed, use wooden blocks to level the implement.

BACK IT UP Put the tractor in its lowest reverse gear. Align the tractor so the top link is squared with the upper connection on the implement, then slowly back the tractor up. When the ends of the lift arms are above the implement pins, slowly lower them into place. Park the tractor and dismount.

HOOK UPHILL FIRST If the implement is slightly off-level, attach the arm on the uphill side first. Get it into place and secure the lynch pin, then move to the downhill side. If it won't fit, try adjusting the tensioners on the tractor's lift arms (older tractors may lack tensioners, but most new ones have them) to provide more or less slack. You can also use a heavy pry bar to slightly move the implement on the opposite side of the offending pin.

HOOK UP THE PTO With the lift-arms attached, hook up the implement's drive shaft (if it has one) to the tractor's PTO shaft. You might need to turn the shaft slightly to align the splines within the drive shaft. Slide the drive shaft onto the PTO shaft, ensuring the detent-style button snaps into place.

HOOK UP THE TOP LINK You might need to adjust the length of the top-link to fit it in place; once it's there, pin it to the implement, tighten it, and you're ready to go.

204 SHARPEN A CHAINSAW

My grandfather was bucking a downed tree in his yard one day when his chainsaw kicked back, buzzing through his collarbone, and narrowly missing both his jugular vein and heart. He survived another 20 years and a second marriage after that mishap, but he never blamed the saw. He insisted that while no chainsaw is safe, a sharp one is at least a little safer because you have to focus on hanging onto it, rather than forcing it through whatever it's cutting.

Sharpen the cutters one at a time using a round sharpening file (found in most hardware stores). It's best to put the bar of the saw in a vise and set the brake to keep the chain from turning, but I've sharpened saws while sitting on a log in the field, too.

The chain will have both right-hand and left-hand cutters, and you'll have to sharpen each side of the chain, one cutter at a time. The cutters have a single-bevel edge, and need only a few strokes, just enough to create a good shine. The chain has one link without a cutter (it's usually painted), as a reference on where to start and end your sharpening procedure.

A properly sharpened saw will cut out long shards of wood (as opposed to fine sawdust) and is a pleasurable tool to wield. Unless, of course, you hang it into your collarbone or leg. Wear proper safety equipment, don't drink and saw, and to maintain your chain, avoid letting it get into the dirt. —W.B.

205 USE A TIRE CHOP-BLOCK

Rednecks hate to toss out used tires because you never know when you might need a couple worn-out KO2s to keep your ride rolling till the next paycheck. But used tires can be put to better use than breeding mosquitoes. Stacked on top of or around a chopping block, those old soldiers will hold wood rounds in place while you work axe magic. You can load the tire with multiple smaller pieces to split, or with one large round to work into quarters. The wood stays in the tire, so you can split smaller and smaller pieces without having to bend over and pick them up each time the axe falls. When the wood splits cleanly, the tire helps keep your axe from biting deeply into the block. Swing wildly and the tire will catch the off-target edge and guard your legs against injury. There are a couple ways to do this, depending on the size of your chopping block.

BUILD A BIG BLOCK Start with a single tire, and use a heavy knife to create four to six 2-inch-wide tabs along the sidewall on the side of the tire that'll face the ground. Cut through the rim bead and a couple of inches into the sidewall, depending on the diameter of your block. Slide the tire onto the top of the block, tabs facing the ground, leaving plenty of tire above the block surface to hold up your wood rounds. Nail the tabs into the side of the chopping block.

SET A SMALLER BLOCK Stack four tires, and place the block in the middle. The top tire needs to extend above the chopping block surface. Tie the tires together with paracord. This arrangement will provide stability for smaller splitting blocks.

206 RIG ANYTHING

Knotcraft is one of those kinds of topics that wise-guy Scoutmasters dreamed up to make everybody else feel stupid. It has its own ridiculous vocabulary (waddaya mean a "bend" is not a "knot"?!), and if you do too much reading on the subject, you'll convince yourself that you have to learn 400 different knots, forget the whole stupid thing, and buy a staple gun and some Gorilla glue instead.

Truth is, aside from fishing, you can get through life knowing only three knots. And, to make them even easier to remember, we're gonna put them in really useful categories, instead of the really stupid categories the Scoutmasters use.

SQUARE KNOT

When you're looking to tie something to something else, you use a square knot. Not a granny knot—and you better know the difference.

STEP 1 Cross two ropes, right rope over left.

STEP 2 Cross them again, left rope over right.

STEP 3 Pull to tighten, and check to make sure each rope enters and exits the knot on the same side.

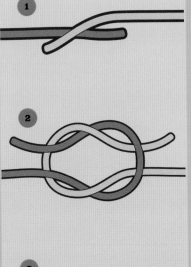

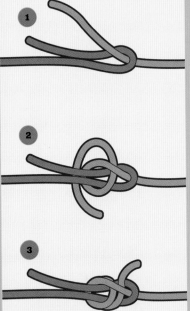

DOUBLE SHEET BEND

When you want to tie a skinny rope to a thick rope because neither is long enough to tie one thing to something else, this is your go-to.

STEP 1 Make a bend in the end of one rope, and pass the end of the second rope through the loop.

STEP 2 Wrap the free end around the loop and under itself twice.

STEP 3 To tighten, hold the first rope and pull the ends of the second rope.

TRUCKER'S HITCH

When you want to secure one thing (say, a mattress) to another thing (say, the roof of an AMC Hornet) so it won't fly off at 90 mph, here's how.

STEP 1 Tie a quick-release loop above any tie-down point, such as a canoe rack.

STEP 2 Run the end of the line around the tie-down and back up through the quick-release loop.

STEP 3 Cinch it down tight. Pinch the rope tightly where it passes through the loop, and finish off the knot with two half-hitches.

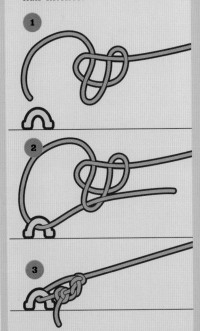

BACK 40

The back 40 is that leftover, unused, catchall little piece of ground that rarely gets plowed or mowed or put to some higher use. It's where the kids go to shoot their BB guns, behind granddaddy's old stepside pickup that's half-covered in blackberry vines. Yours might be a true 40 acres, while mine might be the far corner of the backyard where the johnboat is piled high with 3-D deer targets and the gigging lights. Point is, just about every solid redneck has a little spot set aside for hanging out and piddling with motors and keeping the stuff he can't use right now, but would certainly need the day after he threw it out.

The tips in the following pages aren't leftover and unimportant. They're just hard to stick a label to, so they're here in the back 40, biding their time till the day comes when you have to know how to pick a tick off the dog or get a dead engine started. But be forewarned: The back 40 has a way of sucking you in and not spitting you out till long after dark. —T.E.N.

207 PEE IN A BOTTLE

We hate to get gender-specific, but this is a game-changer for only half the planet. Any man who's been stuck in the top bed in a triple-bunk at deer camp knows that learning to pee in a bottle is one of life's most essential skills. It's not that difficult, and it was a heckuva lot more tricky when all we had was a 20-ounce narrow-necked Cheerwine bottle (though you could indeed argue that Yoo-Hoo bottles were the worst). The invention of wide-mouthed sports drinks bottles made this a snap, so don't chuck that empty Gatorade in the recycling bin quite yet. Here's how it's done in six simple steps:

STEP 1 Roll over on your stomach, then get up on your knees.

STEP 2 Push your bedcovers well out of harm's way.

STEP 3 Activate your Urine Output Device.

STEP 4 Cap the bottle tightly.

STEP 5 Don't forget which bottle it is.

STEP 6 Seriously, don't forget.

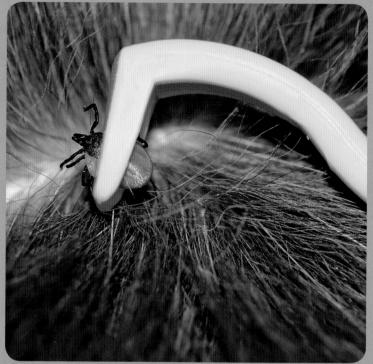

208 PICK A TICK

Hank or George. Dale or Jimmie. There's a lot we might argue over but this much is gospel: Ticks are nasty. They're nasty when they're creepy-crawling under your Fruit of the Looms; they're nasty when they've latched onto the tender tippy-top of your butt crack; and they're for durn sure nasty when they've blown up to the size of a grape and are sticking out of your dog's ear at 2,000,000 PSI and you're going in with a thumb and forefinger.

Growing up, we knew exactly what to do when we got tick bit: We smeared Vaseline on the ticks to suffocate the little S.O.B.s, or we burned their butts with the tip of a hot match because somebody said that would make them back right out. Now we know that all that did was make them vomit more tick goo into our bloodstream.

In these more enlightened, Lyme-ridden days, doctors advise none of the above. Nor do they advise just sucking it up and snatching the ticks off with your fingers. Instead, we are admonished to clean the area around the tick, place the tips of tweezers firmly against the skin, close the tweezers around the tick's mouth, and pull it out. After which, of course, we are advised to clean with rubbing alcohol and first-aid cream, which I never have, and save the tick in a plastic baggie for later identification, which I would never do.

But I have used small fishing pliers and fly-fishing forceps in a pinch. And I've even used light monofilament: Bend it a U shape, slip it over the tick, push it down around the mouth, bend the tick over backwards, and yank like you're pulling out a tooth. This method isn't AMA-approved, but most of the time it will jerk a tick out clean as a whistle. —T.E.N.

209 MAKE A TRUCK STICK

There comes a time when you've had enough crawling into the back of your shell-topped pickup every time you need to find a crescent wrench or that second knee-boot wedged between the dog box and the bag of deer corn. Also, your neighbors are just about done seeing your butt crack. For cryin' out loud, make yourself a truck stick.

Cut a 1½-inch wood rod just a few inches shorter than the length of the truck bed. Drill a pilot hole into the center of one end, and screw in a large vinyl-covered accessory hook (the kind with a large right-angle works better than a round hook). The truck stick stores handily on top of the pickup bed's side wall, where most camper shells are bolted or clamped to the truck via a small, flat shelf. Now you can snag anything while standing at the tailgate, saving your knees and your neighbors' eyes.

210 SIPHON GAS

This method doesn't work with some newer vehicles that come with all sorts of valves and gadgets in the fuel system. But it's the way to go with older cars, boat tanks, four-wheelers, and your granddaddy's 8N Ford.

STEP 1 Scrounge up two lengths of rubber or plastic tubing—old garden hose, surgical tubing, or spare fuel lines will work. You'll need one long enough to reach from an empty gas can into the tank that you're siphoning, and another one long enough to reach from your mouth to the top of gas tank you're borrowing from. Don't worry, this is not the method that requires you to suck gas up the hose.

STEP 2 Stick one end of the long tube into the full gas tank, and place the other end inside the empty gas can. Stick one end of the short tube partway into the gas tank, then fill the space around the two tubes with an old rag to create as tight of a seal as you can.

STEP 3 Blow into the short tube to force pressure into the gas tank and move gas into the long tube. Once the gas is flowing, you can stop blowing.

212 BUILD THE .44 MAGNUM OF BONFIRES

This ain't no weenie roast. The utility of a true bonfire is to sear an awesome night into the memory of everyone in a quarter-mile radius. Go big. But don't go stupid.

STAY SAFE If you're thinking 6-foot logs and spare couches, clear fifty paces between blaze and spectators. Dig a pit a few inches deep, and encircle it in rocks or soil to keep the fire contained and prevent burning logs from rolling into the crowd if the bonfire happens to collapse.

PLAN THE BLAZE To build a fire that goes from a single match to a towering inferno to a contained bed of glowing coals all on its own, start with a 4-foot-tall teepee, with outer logs a good 5 inches thick. Add a towering log cabin around the teepee. Keep every layer as even as possible. If you're really serious, use untreated lumber, or square up or notch the logs so the structure remains largely intact until it collapses on itself.

LIGHT IT UP Everyone's watching, so don't screw it up. Soak a roll of toilet paper in kerosene and tuck it at the base of the fire. You don't have to light it with a flaming arrow shot across the dark sky. But why wouldn't you?

211 DIAGNOSE A DEAD ENGINE

Some people, like my father-in-law, can just look at a dead tractor, truck, or boat motor and just know how to fix it. Mechanics make a living fixing things, and you're permitted to hire one for major work if you don't have the know-how. You might still need to limp your machine home or onto a trailer to get to a mechanic, so keep these two things in mind as you try to get it started.

CHECK THE ELECTRICS If you turn the key and nothing happens at all, the problem is likely electric. Inspect electrical connections, especially battery terminals. Every redneck tool kit ought to have a terminal cleaner, but the edge of a pocketknife will work too. On small gasoline engines, fouled spark plugs can stop the show. If you're removing plugs for inspection, you might as well replace them. The old ones make decent decoy weights.

GIVE IT GAS If the motor cranks but won't run, it's likely a lack of fuel, so check the tank. If it's got fuel, check the fuel delivery system—the lines and intersections that lead to the engine cylinders. They can clog, wear out, or leak. Disconnect them one at a time, pump the throttle, and identify where the stoppage is. More than one engine has been revived by the expulsion of a tiny bit of gunk from a clogged line. —W.B.

213 GET YOUR AXE BACK TO WORK

Just about everyone with a fireplace thinks they know how to sharpen an axe, but the number that have actually tried it is pretty low. The folks at Council Tool Company down in eastern North Carolina's swamp country have been making axes, hatchets, and fire-fighting tools for more than 100 years, and have the drill down tight. For starters, don't bother cranking up your bench grinder. A dry, high-speed grinder will burn the temper out of axe steel, ruining the edge. For sharpening, old-school manual is the only way to go.

STEP 1 Clamp the axe head in a vise (use wood shims or leather to protect it), and get leather gloves and a mill file.

STEP 2 File into the edge of the axe, sharpening on the push stroke, then lift the file off the blade to bring it back to the starting position. Be careful to match the original

grind on the bevel, sharpening the blade's edge to a 25-degree angle.

STEP 3 File until you feel a metal burr on the back side of the blade, then flip the axe head in the vise to file the other side, matching the number of strokes on each side.

STEP 4 Use a hand whetstone in circular motions to remove the final burr.

214 WHITTLE LIKE AN OLD-TIMER

We all like to think we can pick up a hunk of wood and carve a mallard's head, but whittling is one of those things that's about 10 times harder than it looks, so most folks do well to get a pointed stick out of the deal. Follow a few simple guidelines, though, and you should be able to turn a dry branch into a decent faux rifle cartridge in no time flat.

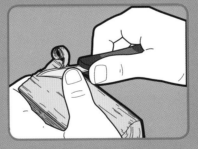

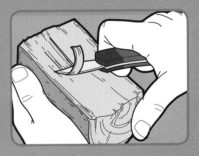

SKIP THE PINE You might think a solid hunk of pine would make for good whittling wood. But fresh pine is packed with sap and sticky pitch, which make it hard to get a knife through cleanly and a little unsafe for beginners. If it's gotta be pine, make sure it's seasoned so it's not so sappy. Even better, head to a craft store and pick up a few pieces of basswood. It's pretty soft, like pine, but without the sap and grain that can make for difficult carving.

GIVE IT A PUSH You won't get far with the standard pencil-sharpening stroke. The push stroke is a whittler's take on the standard, but has greater power and control. If you're right-handed, hold the wood in your left hand and knife in your right. Place the knife's edge on the wood, facing away. Line up both thumbs on the spine of the knife blade, and push the blade forward with your left thumb, using your right fingers and thumb to guide the blade for the desired cut.

PULL INSTEAD The pare cut is a pulling stroke, like you might use to pare an apple. With the wood in your left hand, hold the knife in your right hand with the edge facing you, and your right thumb against the wood. Use thumb pressure to guide the knife blade while drawing in the fingers of your right hand. This pulls the blade into the wood for short, precise strokes.

215 DECORATE WITH DEER ANTLERS

Just because your last deer wasn't a Booner doesn't mean it can't be the center of attention. Here's how to turn a buck's headgear into household items that you definitely won't find at IKEA.

HOLD TOILET PAPER Grind a flat spot on the back of the antler, and bolt the thing to the wall. The trick is to cut or grind down the tips so you can squeeze a roll into an oblong shape and slip the tube over the branched antlers. When the roll regains its original shape, it won't slip off when you're unspooling a handful.

STOW TOOTHPICKS Cut a 3-inch section of thick antler, secure it in a vise, and bore out the center with a large drill bit. Smooth with steel wool and varnish. Is there a better redneck gift for groomsmen? Yes, but several sets of 35-inch Boggers won't leave much for the honeymoon.

MAKE A KNIFE HANDLE This isn't the Bowie knife you wear to the store or use to stick a bayed-up hog. No, this one hangs on the wall. The antler pedicle will be the base, maybe embellished by a brass pommel, and it will be polished to a smooth taper right into the guard. The finest examples will have a wildlife scene painted on the blade.

SCRATCH YOUR BACK Affix a single antler from a basket-racked buck to the end of a ½-inch dowel rod with some leather lashing and a drop or two of super glue. It's perfect for really getting at that chigger rash in the low, sweaty part of your back that you'd just as soon not touch with your hands on a sultry July afternoon.

BLEACH A SKULL Rednecks across the pond had it right when they began bleaching skulls. A European mount provides a vibrant contrast between the bone and antler. It's cheaper than a shoulder mount, and it makes a far better centerpiece for Christmas dinner.

216 SPIT ON THE FIRE

An accurate stream of tobacco juice across hot campfire coals is like a physical exclamation point to a good story. "It was the biggest buck I'd ever seen." Spit, sizzle. Do it right, and the stream will be narrow and forceful, emit a single-note sound, and make your preceding statement downright biblical. Do it wrong, and brown saliva will end up all over your chin and shirt, and your cover will be blown.

First, allow a good mouth full of saliva to pool under your tongue. Tilt your chin down, build up a bit of pressure, raise your tongue a bit, purse your lips, and let fly. Your bottom lip should protrude slightly. Don't think of it like spitting out something that tastes bad. It's more like spitting water-gun style. Aiming is instinctive and improves with practice.

217 MAKE A BEER-CAN SPITTOON

Aluminum cans are good for holding beer and Mountain Dew, but they make terrible spittoons since the rim around the top tends to fill up with 'baccer juice. The best solution is to find a plastic bottle with a screw-on cap. If there's nothing but cans available, modify yours by first breaking off the tab, and then dropping it into the bottom of the can. Next, use the pommel of your Bowie knife to smash open the mouth of the can so that your spit port is nearly as wide as the can itself. Finally, use the dull side of your blade to bend over the jagged aluminum so you don't cut your lip. You're now ready for a good chaw.

218 STOCK A REDNECK MAMA'S TOOLKIT

Let us celebrate Mama, the most sacred redneck of them all. From cooking dinner to fixing what's broken to administering discipline (all three of which are frequently done at once), every Mama needs a tool kit. Here's a look at some of the crucial items.

SQUEEZE BUTTER It'll grease a skillet and spread easily across biscuits. Kids love the farting noises that it makes when near empty.

HAMBURGER HELPER Pair it with any ground meat—from venison to beef to goat—for a quick and nourishing meal.

FLY SWATTER Makes unruly toddlers and coon dogs listen every time.

COOL WHIP TUBS Redneck mamas might accept Tupperware at Christmas, but her cabinets are full of these.

BOXED WHITE ZINFANDEL Mama's medicine at the end of a tough day of raisin'.

FOLDING CAMP CHAIRS Whether the family's coming over, a ball game's on the schedule, or Mama just needs a quiet moment to herself in the yard, camp chairs will deliver.

MULTI-TOOL Mama might need to open a can of beans, change a clothes dryer fuse, and assemble a Power Wheels Jeep all in the same day. With this, she can.

YOGA PANTS Not for working out—for the fact they always fit no matter what. Plus, they nicely display that tattoo she just paid off.

CIGARETTE PURSE Even if Mama gave up the menthols, she still carries her phone, credit cards, and .380 auto in this.

WIRE COAT HANGERS From triple layering her "winter stuff" to unclogging sink drains, wire hangers do jobs in ways plastic hangers simply cannot.

219 ROCK CROCS WITH PRIDE

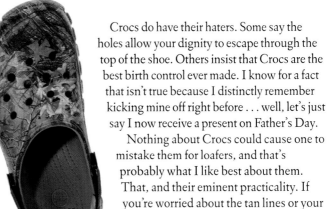

In those rare instances when boots aren't required, Crocs are the standard-issue footwear of the redneck. These foam slip-ons are available in a variety of colors, but that doesn't matter—yours should be camouflage.

My Crocs have been so soaked in catfish slime and carp blood that I've had to slosh them around in lake water for several seconds before putting them back on. I've worn them in treestands and ground blinds, while sneaking up on squirrels, wading creeks, mowing the lawn, and working in the garden. The holes in the tops of them leave tan lines on your feet reminiscent of the pox. They say to everyone: "I go outside."

Crocs do have their haters. Some say the holes allow your dignity to escape through the top of the shoe. Others insist that Crocs are the best birth control ever made. I know for a fact that isn't true because I distinctly remember kicking mine off right before . . . well, let's just say I now receive a present on Father's Day.

Nothing about Crocs could cause one to mistake them for loafers, and that's probably what I like best about them. That, and their eminent practicality. If you're worried about the tan lines or your dignity, just pair them with shin-high wool socks, same as I do throughout the cool-season months. —W.B.

220 LEARN SKINNY DIPPING 101

It's not exactly one of the seven deadly sins, but cavorting in a farm pond or river slough while wearing your birthday suit ranks high on the list of redneck guilty pleasures. Here are the answers to some commonly asked—or at least, thought of—questions for those special times when a full moon swim seems like the right thing to do.

CAN I JUST WATCH? No. This is not a spectator sport. Watching from the bank marks you as a weakling and, frankly, a little weird. If you're not into the Garden of Eden thing, head back up to the road and keep the truck heater running for the true athletes.

WILL I CATCH WORMS? Possibly. No. Almost impossible. Really, totally unlikely. This is akin to asking, "Won't a snake bite me?" Just because you're naked as a newborn doesn't mean you should act like one.

WHAT DO I LOOK AT? Now we get to the nuts and bolts of the matter. Having decided to strip and swim, how do you deal with the carnal landscape? Sure, you've been dreaming of taking a gander at Clarice since your Bible School vacation. But a creek-side cavort is not a peep show. Look her in the eyes when she's talking to you. Leer unto others as ye would have them leer unto your own PBR-and-gas-station-burrito-sculpted self.

WILL SOMEONE TAKE MY CLOTHES? Every dipstick in the world thinks it's hilarious to run off with that pile of jorts and tightie-whities left on the dock. My rule of thumb: My drawers go in the drink with me. I don't fully disrobe—or de-pant—until I'm in the water.

WHAT ELSE SHOULD I KNOW TO PREPARE FOR? Monitor bean intake during skinny dip season. It's not a bubble bath. —T.E.N.

221 DIVERSIFY YOUR REDNECK PORTFOLIO

Like any good portfolio, redneck investments are diverse and thoroughly planned. Whether you're looking to invest a leaf or a full head of presidential cabbage, here's a look at what's hot at the time of this book's writing.

YOU HAVE	YOU BUY	WHY?
$25	Genuine: The Alan Jackson Story Box Set	Because you're dang right, it's alright to be little bitty.
$100	A 26-Quart Ozark Trail Cooler	Because you'd like a Yeti, but Wal-Mart doesn't sell them. And you still have to spring for that new alternator.
$500	20 rolls of Copenhagen	Because when your wife runs out of her mint pouches and needs to bum a dip, you'll always have enough to share.
$1,500	An X15 Flamethrower	Because those zombies aren't going to incinerate themselves. (Please note, using a flamethrower is illegal in the state of California. Even against zombies.)
$4,000	Yourself a $4,000 gift card to the taxidermist	Because there's no better way to kick off hunting season than with $4,000 worth of irrational confidence.
$8,000	A Wilson Combat Pinnacle 1911 .45 ACP	Because you plan to win the "prettiest gun" contest at this year's family reunion/cookout/pistol match. Show a little class, and spring for something nicer than a nylon holster.

PAINT YOUR TRUCK CAMO

We'd hunted that morning, and were wore out from a long walk out of the beaver swamp. Sitting on my duplex porch listening to the truck engine tick and hiss, we hadn't given a single thought to what we were going to do with the next 8 hours of daylight. That's a luxury you have when you're in your 20s, working a pretty good job, and you haven't yet fallen under the spell of the wedding preacher. I think this was during the short October wood duck season, but I'm not sure. Can't recall if we killed any ducks that morning or not, nor where we hunted. But I very well remember the moment my buddy Lee Davis set down his spit cup and spoke a word of prophecy.

"One of these days," Lee reckoned, "we ought to paint that truck camo."

I sat bolt upright in the straight-back rocker. There are moments in life that flash like lightning, and you know you should act fast before you think too hard. This was one of them.

"Let's do it," I replied. We were at the hardware store in less than 5 minutes.

That was my first pickup. I'd paid $500 for it when $500 could get me through a month. My mom brokered the deal with a guy on the construction site where she worked as secretary. The rig was a white 1973 Chevrolet Silverado with a long bed, beat-up camper shell, and 3-on-the-tree transmission. Corrosion had eaten the fender wells, and some spots on the floor were so rusted out you could you see the road under your feet. But she started every time, got pretty good mud traction with the shell's weight, and she was all mine.

"What you painting?" asked the clerk at the register when I asked where they kept the spray paint. I suspect he figured I was working on some respectable project, like an iron fence or outdoor table.

"That truck right there," I told him, nodding through the storefront glass. He jerked his thumb towards the back of the store and excused himself. Lee and I just about cleared the place out of Rustoleum in the four colors of the redneck rainbow: green, brown, black, and primer.

Ninety minutes later, we were done. We hadn't had a plan or a pattern, though Lee cut some leaf stencils out of a cardboard box that turned out pretty nice. Most importantly, we didn't have anybody looking over our shoulders and sniffing, "Y'all ought not do that."

Everybody loved that camo pickup truck, except maybe the neighbors. People would honk and wave, folks would turn their heads on the sidewalks, and I could hear what they all were thinking: "Dang. I wish I had a camo truck."

Julie and I were dating pretty heavy by then, so I knew she wouldn't just break it off outright. But that truck was my sole transportation, and she didn't fully buy into the awesomeness of a 15-year-old pickup in DIY Realtree. But she had her own sweet ride, an Oldsmobile Cutlass Supreme coupe with a 3-speed manual that would bark tread like a beagle pack, so it was something to drive on dates until I got a red S-10 Blazer with power windows and everything. Marriage followed closely, so you know where this is going.

I don't have many regrets, but selling that truck is high on the list. A tatted-up bricklayer bought it for $350. But for a few glorious years that truck embodied a certain approach to this business of life: Anything worth doing is worth doing right now before somebody hears about it and ruins your moment of inspiration.

And don't ever let anyone ever tell you "primer" isn't a color. —T.E.N.

INDEX

ABOUT THE AUTHORS

WILL BRANTLEY is the hunting editor of *Field & Stream*, where he handles much of the brand's hunting content, both on paper and online. He even manages to write a fishing story or two each spring. Brantley has been an *F&S* staffer for nearly three years, and was a full-time freelancer and regular contributor for seven years prior to that. He's written for most of the major hook-and-bullet titles, including *Outdoor Life, Ducks Unlimited,* and *American Hunter.* Brantley grew up in western Kentucky, and that's where he lives today with his wife, son, and a semi-crazy Catahoula cur. He maintains two small farms and hunts and fishes for whatever is in season.

T. EDWARD NICKENS is editor-at-large of *Field & Stream*, where he's spent nearly 20 years as the title's squirrel expert. That's not really a full-time gig, though, so he's also written for less rednecky titles, like *Garden & Gun, Smithsonian,* and *National Geographic Adventure.* Nickens has hunted and fished everywhere from the Nicaraguan rainforest to the Arctic Sea—trips from which he gleaned material for his two earlier *Field & Stream* books, *The Total Outdoorsman Manual* and *The Total Outdoorsman: Skills & Tools.* He's also hosted the television shows *The Gun Nuts* and *The Total Outdoorsman Challenge* on the Outdoor Channel. He is a native of the northern province of Cackalacky.

ACKNOWLEDGEMENTS

WILL BRANTLEY

Thanks to Mariah Bear and the Weldon Owen staff for the effort that went into this book. Thank you to my colleagues at *F&S*, especially Deputy Editor Dave Hurteau, who was the first to suggest a book called, "The Total Redneck Manual." And, of course, thanks to my partner in crime, T. Edward Nickens. Buddy, you've long been one of my favorite authors, and it's an honor to share a byline with you. Finally, thank you to Dad, Bobby, Ronnie, Donald, Larry, Kenny, and so many other genuine rednecks for teaching me all that you have.

This one is dedicated to Anse and his mama. He's my little redneck in the making, and she's my queen.

T. EDWARD NICKENS

This is my third book in the "Total Outdoorsman" series, and the inimitable Mariah Bear has been a constant support from the start. Thanks, Mariah, for helping reinvent the wheel! The staff at Field & Stream loves a good story, and I appreciate editor-in-chief Colin Kearns for allowing me to slip my leash every now and then. Working with Will Brantley has been a kick, and I will forever be in awe at how the man can create artful prose on subjects that involve sticking your hand in places it ought not to be.

And of course, to my family. My kids—daughter Markie and son Jack—are old enough to wonder how they're going to live this book down. But that will only last until they need allowance. And to my bride of a quarter-century-plus, Julie. Well, sweetie, you knew what you were getting into that day I spray-painted my truck camouflage. And you've got to give me credit—it's been ages since I asked you to fix me a spit cup.

ABOUT THE MAGAZINE

In every issue of *Field & Stream* you'll find a lot of stuff: beautiful photography and artwork, adventure stories, wild game recipes, humor, commentary, reviews, and more. That mix is what makes the magazine so great, what's helped it remain relevant since 1895. But at the heart of every issue are the skills. The tips that explain how to land a big trout, the tactics that help you shoot the deer of your life, the lessons that teach you how to survive a cold night outside—those are the stories that readers have come to expect from *Field & Stream*.

You'll find a ton of those skills in *The Total Redneck Manual*, but much as we may try to deny it, there are a few interesting and useful skills thatdon't quite fall into this book's subject matter. And anyway, o whether you're new to hunting and fishing or an old pro, there's always more to learn. You can continue to expect *Field & Stream* to teach you those essential skills in every issue. Plus, there's all that other stuff in the magazine, too, which is pretty great. To order a subscription, visit www.fieldandstream.com/subscription.

ABOUT THE WEBSITE

When *Field & Stream* readers aren't hunting or fishing, they kill hours (and hours) on www.fieldandstream.com. And once you visit the site, you'll understand why.

First, if you enjoy the skills in this book, there's plenty more online—both within our extensive archives of stories from the writers featured here, as well as our network of 50,000-plus experts who can answer all of your questions about the outdoors.

At Fieldandstream.com, you'll get to explore the world's largest online destination for hunters and anglers. Our blogs, written by the leading experts in the outdoors, cover every facet of hunting and fishing and provide constant content that instructs, enlightens, and always entertains. Our collection of adventure videos contains footage that's almost as thrilling to watch as it is to experience for real. And our photo galleries include the best wildlife and outdoor photography you'll find anywhere.

Perhaps best of all is the community you'll find at Fieldandstream.com. It's where you can argue with other readers about the best whitetail cartridge or the perfect venison chili recipe. It's where you can share photos of the fish you catch and the game you shoot. It's where you can enter contests to win guns, gear, and other great prizes. And it's a place where you can spend a lot of time sharing your very own redneck wisdom. Which is OK. Just make sure to reserve some hours for the outdoors, too.

CREDITS

TEXT

Will Brantley: 4, 7, Skin a Squirrel, 15, Skin a Rabbit, 16, 18, What's a Holler?, 19, 20, 21, 22, 23, 24, 25, 36, 37, 38, 39, 40, Skin a Mountain Lion, 42, 43, 44, 46, 47, 49, 50, 51, 52, 54, 55, 56, 60, 66, 68, 71, 72, 74, 78, 80, 81, 82, 83, 84, 86, 88, 89, 90, 91, 93, What's a Sac-a-Lait?, 95, 96, 97, 98, Scale a Bream, 101, 104, 105, 107, 108, 110, 111, 112, 113, 114, 115, 119, What's a Fiddler?, 120, 123, 127, 128, 129, 130, 131, 132, 133, 136, 156, 157, 158, 159, Clean a Northern Pike, 160, 161, 162, 163, 164, 170, 171, 173, 174, 175, 176, 177, 180, 183, 188, 189, 190, 195, 200, 201, 202, 203, 204, 211, 216, 217, 218, 219, 220

T. Edward Nickens: 1, 2, 3, 5, 6, 8, 9, 10, 11, 12, 13, 14, 17, 26, 27, 28, 29, 30, 31, 32, 33, 34, 35, 41, 45, 48, 53, 57, 58, 59, 61, 62, 63, 64, 65, 67, 69, 70, 73, 74, 75, 76, 77, Clean a Duck, 79, 85, Skin a Snake, 87, 92, 94, 99, 100, 103, 102, 106, 109, 116, 117, 118, Skin a Catfish, 121, 122, 124, 125, 126, 134, 135, 137, 138, 139, 140, 141, 142, 143, 144, 145, 146, 147, 148, 149, 150, 151, 152, 153, 154, 155, 165, 166, 167, What's a Snakehead?, 168, 169, 171, 176, 178, 179, 181, 182, 183, 184, 185, 186, 187, 191, 192, 193, 194, 195, 196, 197, 198, 199, 205, 206, 207, 208, 209, 210, 212, 213, 214, 215, 221

PHOTOGRAPHY

Barry Blackburn / Shutterstock.com: 197 (ketchup); **Hollis Bennett:** 162 (bottom); **Will Brantley:** "Big Game" (right), 38, Getting The Moose Home", 80, 89, 95, "Catfish" (right), 112, 113, Snakes And Smallmouths", "Trash Fish" (left), 160, "On the Farm", 201, 203, "Paint Your Truck Camo", Index; **Denver Bryan:** 74; **Cabela's:** 19, 23, 101, 104, 120 (middle left, bottom left), 141, 159, 219; **Buck USA:** 191; **Chris Chrisman:** 14, "Block Out For Bushytails", 17; **Rob Dolgaard and Suzi Hutsell:** 190; **Engbretson Underwater Photography:** 108, 138, 147, 154; **Tom Fowlks:** 57; **Toni Genes / Shutterstock.com:** 188; **Russell Graves:** Small Game Introduction (right), 18, "Don't Steal Your Pregnant Wife's Buck", 51, "Upland Birds" (right), 68, 77, "Work For Ducks", "Take A Kid Frog Giggin'", "Panfish" (left), 106, "Bass" (right), 123, 136, 145; **John Hafner:** Contents, "Big Game" (right), 30, 39, 40, 46, 49, 50, 63, 71; **Brent Humphreys:** "Parenting" (right); **International Game Fish Association:** 158 (all); **Erika Larsen:** 45; **Justin Leesmann:** 167; **Colby Lynse:** Fishing Introduction, "Get Serious About Panfish", 142; **Mepps:** 8; **Mlenny / iStock:** 171; **T. Edward Nickens:** Contents (Bronco), Hunting Introduction, 13, 29, 32, 35, 69, "Waterfowl" (both), 73, 75, 79, "Panfish" (right), Trout (left), "Cooking & Drinking" (both), "Guns & Knives" (left), "Paint Your Truck Camo," Closing Page; **Redshad.com:** 125; **Dan Saelinger:** 91; **Shutterstock:** Half Title, Title Page, Magazine INtro, Contents (man with fish), Contents (boy on ATV), "What Is A Redneck?", Hunting Opener, "Small Game" (left), 2, 3, 7, 10, 11, 16, 20, 21, 24, 31, 36, 42, 43, 55, 56, 60, 62, "Upland Birds" (left), 64, 75 (4 inset images), 78, "Shoot Some Varmints" (both), 82, 83, 84, 87, 88, Fishing Opener, 91, "Sac-a-lait", 94, 99, 100, 105, 110, 118, 119, 120 (top left, top right, bottom right), 122 (all), "Bass" (left), 124, 127, 128, 129, 130, 131, 135, "Trout" (right), 140 (all), 143, 146, 150, 152 (all). "Trout Fishing with Kenny Dean", "Fish With Teeth" (both), 153, 155, 157, 159 (left), "Learn To Love Trash" (right), 162 (top, middle), 163, 165, Everything Else Opener, Everything Else Introduction, "Parenting" (left), "Snakehead",168, 171 (both), 172, 173, 175, 176 (both), 179, 180, 184, 185, 186, 187, 189, 190, 191 (all), "Don't Burn Down the Dorm", "Guns & Knives" (right), 195, 197 (all), 199, "On The Farm", 204, Back 40 (both), 207, 208, 211, 212, 213, 218, 220, 221, Credits Page, Colophon; **Dusan Smetana:** 41; **Keith Sutton:** "Catfish", 107; **Trip Advisor:** "Fiddler"; **War Eagle Boats:** 164; **Wikicommons:** "Warble", 192

ILLUSTRATION

Conor Buckley: 08, 25, 48, 54, 61, 65, 81, 100, 111, 114, 116, 133, 137,151,156, 178, 182, 193, 195, 196, 206, 209, 210, 215, 216; **Hayden Foell:** 17, 43, 71, 97, 205, Hell I can Skin That: Rabbits; **Ryan Kirby:** 90; **Vic Kulihin:** 47, 85, Hell I can Skin That: Mountain Lion, Duck, Rattlesnake, Hell I can Clean That: Pike; **Raymond Larrett:** 06, 09; **Dan Marsiglio:** 117; **Christine Meighan:** 01, 04, 22, 70, 72, 166, 214, Hell I can Scale That: Bream, Catfish; **Robert L. Prince:** 05, 34; **Mike Sudal:** 12, 134; **Lauren Towner:** 11, 28, 53, 75, 93, 126, 139;

weldon**owen**

President & Publisher Roger Shaw
SVP Sales & Marketing Amy Kaneko
Associate Publisher Mariah Bear
Project Editor J.T. Browning
Associate Editor Ian Cannon
Creative Director Kelly Booth
Art Director Allister Fein
Illustration Coordinator Conor Buckley
Production Director Michelle Duggan
Imaging Manager Don Hill

Weldon Owen would also like to thank Brittany Bogan
and Marisa Solis for editorial assistance and Ken
Dellapenta for the index.

CAMERON + COMPANY

Publisher Chris Gruener
Managing Editor Jan Hughes
Creative Director Iain R. Morris
Art Director Suzi Hutsell
Designer Rob Dolgaard

Weldon Owen is a division of Bonnier Publishing USA
1045 Sansome Street #100
San Francisco, CA 94111
www.weldonowen.com

ISBN 978-168188-242-0
10 9 8 7 6 5 4 3 2 1
2017 2018 2019 2020 2021
Printed in China by 1010 Printing International

FIELD& STREAM

Editorial Director Anthony Licata
Editor-in-Chief Colin Kearns
Group Creative Director Sean Johnston
Managing Editor Jean McKenna
Deputy Editors Dave Hurteau, Slaton L. White
Copy Chief Donna L. Ng
Fishing Editor Joe Cermele
Hunting Editor Will Brantley
Associate Editor JR Sullivan
Editorial Assistant Hilary Ribons
Photography Director John Toolan
Art Director Brian Struble
Associate Art Directors Russ Smith, James A. Walsh
Production Manager Judith Weber
Digital Director Nate Matthews
Online Content Editor Alex Robinson
Associate Online Editor JR Sullivan
Special Projects Editor Mike Toth

2 Park Avenue
New York, NY 10016
www.fieldandstream.com